Harmony in Relationships

Add love and respect in your relationships!

Padmapriya Mahendarkar

ISBN: 978-1-7370360-1-2 (Paperback)

The information given in this book should not be treated as a substitute for professional medical advice; always consult a medical practitioner. Any use of information in this book is at the reader's discretion and risk. Neither the author nor the publisher can be held responsible for any loss, claim or damage.

Book cover image "Beige Green Poppy Flower background"
Book design created through www.canva.com

First published by Clean Intellect Publishing 2021

This book is dedicated to

Dadi Janki

Former Administrative Head of Brahma Kumaris

Table of Contents

Each article in this book contributes to building understanding, love, respect and harmony in relationships. Reflection is provided at end of each topic. Write them in your personal journal. For any questions or queries, feel free to email at bksisterpriya@gmail.com

Being Nice No Matter What

We would have heard the word "nice" many times and used it ourselves many times in our life. We do feel good when someone is nice to us and when something nice happens to us. We also do our best to be nice with everyone.

We find it easy to be nice with someone who is sweet to us. But it's quite challenging to still be nice with someone who is giving us hard time. Being nice is to be sweet, genuine, kind, loving, caring, courteous and compassionate.

How to be nice?
1. Understanding each person is different and has a unique script to play/enact.
Example: "I can only control my thoughts, words and actions and not that of others."

2. Accept others wholeheartedly.
Example: "Like I accept the flowers and thorns of a rose plant; I accept every human being as they are!"

3. Respecting the differences and defects of others.
Example: I need to respect their rejection or anger. Even if it's negative; I still need to respect it as they are playing their part in this world. Good or bad, it is a part.

4. Giving space for that person to play their script.

Example: Being non-judgmental and not exercising control. Letting them be and do what they want to.

5. Take cover of the self, i.e., protecting the inner being.
Example: Not getting hurt, not taking sorrow through assumptions and imaginations.

6. Live Beyond.
Example: not complaining, worrying, and gossiping about others

7. Sending good wishes to others , i.e., think well for them if it's possible for me.
Example: "I wish you peace of mind," "I wish you understanding and clarity," and "I love you irrespective of your weaknesses."

8. Practicing to be nice and sweet towards them.
I need not get involved with them but I can just smile when I bump into them rather than giving a stern face or an upset look. Basically I clean my heart, i.e., I try not to hold onto the rude behaviors of the person in order for me to be genuinely nice towards them.

Sometimes I need time to completely let go of certain behaviors of others since they could be very deep and devastating. In that case, I take a gentle slow step of healing inside and I choose to fake it until I make it as I value the importance of being nice to others.

Why should I be nice?

1. If I am not nice; say I yell when I am being yelled at. I create a non-ending circle of negative karma (cause and effect of actions). Irrespective of anyone's behavior towards me, the Universal Law of Karma teaches me to be peaceful, loving and non-violent.

2. If I react and just show off my hurt or retaliation to others who are not nice to me then I need to face the consequences of my reactions too. I may have to pay the price for hurting others.

Example: Say you hate your colleague for whatever reason. The hatred is felt more strongly by the source (you) than the receiver. Just like the song that is played in loudspeakers; the further the distance the lesser the sound you hear. The closer you are to the speakers, the more you feel the loudness.

3. If I am nice, I am safeguarding myself. I do not stress my being. Even though my reactions of anger, sadness, arguing, blaming are automatic, if I take a moment to pause and choose to be still calm. I can feel the freedom in my atmosphere and relationships. I do not feel guilty of anything and I give room for other person to get back to me whenever they are ready.

Why others are not nice with me?

Do you beat yourself with these questions?
- Why they are mean to me?
- Why they are nice to everyone except me?

In spirituality we learn; each person is unique and have their choices of actions good or bad. When I know my inner being, I am empowered and I start giving rather than taking.

As long as this inner work of self-love and self-respect is pending, I will always tend to hurt and get hurt. Basically when a person's behavior is rude; it means that person is not connected with their true self. So I need to feel compassion for them instead of anger. When I am in link with my own inner self, I am only full of peace, love, wisdom and happiness. Nothing else... and I will radiate those qualities no matter what...

Reflection:
1. Do I hurt others? Let me write the names of people whom I don't treat well and why?
2. What change I can bring in my attitude and behavior?
3. Let go of all my judgements for one day and write the observations.

Om Shanti (I am peace)

Dealing with Difficult People

Difficult people are those people who are,
1. Give hard time
2. Grumpy
3. Bully
4. Angry and frustrated
5. Less tolerant
6. Rude and mean
7. Difficult to communicate with
8. Bad listeners
9. Argue a lot
10. Giving the silent treatment

Basically they are people who are not sweet and are not easy to work with. Difficult people are called difficult as their behavior causes distress to others.

Two Categories of Difficult People:
Category 1: There are people who are generally difficult for everyone to work with.
Example: People who are short tempered.
Category 2: You find difficulty working with certain people but others find them ok or even great.
Example: People who are mean to you but they are nice with others.

It is quite easy to point fingers at others. No matter how difficult someone may be, you hold total responsibility for your happiness in life and no one can snatch it from you unless you allow them.

There are two solutions for working with difficult people.
Solution 1: Understanding Difficult people
Generally, when we come into contact with a person, we form impressions based on their behavior. We only see the surface but not what's beneath it.

Each behavior is caused by an attitude, thought and feeling. Negative behavior is caused by emotions like fear, anger, jealousy, and ego. Say if someone is rude to you, it means they might be insecure, jealous or egoistic.

Practice:
Hunt for the hidden emotion or cause in any situation.
- Clear your mind.
- Don't take things personally.
- Ask yourself what is causing this person to behave like that?
- What are they holding inside?
- How is it connected with me? Am I even connected with their behavior?

You may not believe it, most of the times it's not you. It's just their habits, personality or their own problems in their life that makes them difficult to work with. Difficult people tend to project their emotions towards others. As they cannot process within, they tend to blame people around them.

Example 1:
Your boss gets mad at you for no reason.
The background cause for this reaction is not you or your work but just he had a bad day with his/her family.
There are two reasons for this;
1. The boss finds you as a place of his/her emotional release and an easy means of projecting his/her emotions since you can't/don't react back.
You can stop being a victim and just shake off your boss's behavior. You can stop taking sorrow, stay in your power and listen with great compassion. When you start doing this, your boss can no longer project his/her emotions since you won't be a good receiver anymore. Difficult people bully only weak ones.

Example 2:
Your boss does not like you for some reason. Your boss is judgmental of you in terms of cultural differences, racism or discrimination of any type.
Instead of saying, "Poor Me! Or Why Me?" I can reduce my expectation that my boss should always like me or treat me well. I can become a master and build my
Self-esteem and stop looking for an approval.

This might be hard initially but if I practice, it is possible.
I cannot change my boss but I can adjust my attitude and responses. Rather than taking sorrow, I can be understanding

and compassionate. This way I create a protective shield for my own feelings from being hurt by difficult people around me.

The Truth:
In fact, difficult people are sadder than everyone. Any type of difficulty they cause to others is due to their fear or insecurity. They don't feel happiness and contentment in life since they get what they give (Karma.) You can substitute the word "boss" for any person whom you find difficulty with; it may be a child/family/friend.

While Making Mistakes:
When we make mistakes, it is quite difficult to face others as we fear their reactions. We become vulnerable to face them especially when the other is strict and has zero tolerance. In their presence, there is no room for mistakes.

If a mistake did happen, I struggle with their outbursts and meanness. I also might find their reaction overwhelming to deal with. In such scenarios I need to take things lightly and accept their behavior without judgment. I let go of the idea of them treating me in a gentle way like I would do.

Since mistakes cannot be controlled, Mistakes happen!
The only option is to handle them in an easy way without taking things personally. This way I don't get hurt and feel bad for my mistakes through them. Difficult people hurt us harder even for small things as they want you to feel bad and awful! Remember; each person in this world is unique and special in

their own way. I protect myself by allowing them to play their part as it is.

I do not force them to change nor do I become a victim!

How difficult people become difficult?
They weren't born difficult. They just developed that personality due to their bad experiences. It might be from their childhood conditioning or a learned behavior.

Difficult people also need help and support from us. They are rude and manipulative as they are needy of peace, love and happiness. When I develop kindness and compassion, I can tolerate, be patient and forgive them rather than blaming them. I can give instead of expecting!

Reflection:
1. Write the names and behaviors of two people whom you find difficult to work with.
2. Instead of blaming them, what responsibility you can take to improve the situation?
3. How can you protect yourself while being attacked?

Om Shanti (I am peace)

Personality Types

We are all knitted together in different personalities which we carry from birth or develop as we grow. Each one of us is unique and special in our own way yet our comfort zone lies in our personalities. By understanding one's personality, it's easier to build a relationship with the self in that angle and tune to our true divine personality from that space.

By understanding others' personalities, it makes us free from annoying and banging our heads as to why people act in a certain way and why they are like that. This knowledge helps us to interact and relate with others as they are and be compassionate to one another.

The below distinction of personalities are only on personal observation and means no offense to any individual.
1. Expressive, Active Aggressive and Clean
2. Expressive, Active Aggressive and Revengeful
3. Quiet, Passive Aggressive and Revengeful
4. Quiet, Passive Aggressive and Neutral
5. Spiritual or Divine Personality

Expressive, Active Aggressive Description:
Expressive:
They can express themselves very well, i.e., convey their thoughts, feelings, emotions and ideas without any hesitation to another individual. They are excellent communicators,

outgoing and straight forward. They will be the first ones to initiate a conversation and the one who speaks a lot in any discussion, shooting ideas, debating, sharing and so on.

Active Aggressive:
As they are transparent in expressing their likes/dislikes, emotions, judgments and basically anything going in their heart/intellect without much filtering, they might sometimes end up hurting others.

They are strong personalities and can be controlling dominant at times.

Type 1 Expressive, Active Aggressive and Clean:
Even though they hurt the people around them, once their head is cooled down they rush for forgiveness. They quickly go into guilt mode recapping their behavior and tend to fix the relationship again and show concern about others. They are the ones who apologize sincerely realizing that they were harsh. They do not hold anything in their heart. One moment they are mad at you, next moment they completely let go of it and treat you nice.

Type 2 Expressive, Active Aggressive and Revengeful:
They are expressive and active aggressive but they are the ones who become revengeful and egoistic.
As they can't let go of their madness, they will be constantly mean, rude and boss you around. Their ego is hurt and they can't handle it without projecting it on others. They are the "grumpy" people who don't repair or care about others' feelings after being expressive of their negative emotions.

Quiet and Passive Aggressive Description:
Quiet:
They are generally calm, quiet, withdrawn and observant.
They do not express their feelings easily. They process their
thoughts slowly and reactions come out passively and
sometimes indirectly. They have immense patience and
tolerance. They show respect to others by listening without
arguing with them. They do not orally hurt others.

Passive Aggressive:
Because they do not easily express, they tend to suppress their
emotions. This habit can harm the self and one day might
explode in a large scale. Due to the quiet nature, they might
easily become a victim and get exploited by active aggressive
souls.

Type 3 Quiet, Passive Aggressive and Revengeful:
Unlike active aggressive, when this type gets hurt by the other
they exhibit their emotions in an indirect manner like silent
treatment, avoiding eye contact, gossip, rejection and back
stabbing. They might treat you sweetly with smile but in their
hearts, they hold grudges and take revenge.

They can also be deceptive and one is able to figure out things
with them only by sensing their feelings and vibrations as
open communication doesn't work with them.

They would dispute that everything is okay but never openly
discuss the subject with you. Passive Aggressive people do

hurt the other person profoundly and sometimes leave the other no choice as nothing is dealt directly. Such situations can be more tricky and painful as they cannot be confronted easily.

Type 4 Quiet, Passive Aggressive and Neutral:
They do not even care about revenge. They just ignore if anything happens in relationships. They are in their own world and do not want to go into the drama of fighting active/ passive. They are mostly self-oriented and have enough experience with such games and so they prefer to remain detached. This way they take care of their emotional self and do not obviously create any direct karma with other souls.

They do not have any specific negative or positive feelings towards people who have disputes with them. They just go beyond and let people do whatever they wanted to. This sort of behavior may annoy the other person much further because all human beings expect a reaction directly or indirectly.

Type 4 personality is adopted by some people from their past bad experiences. Yet every type of personality hurts each other in a direct or indirect manner. Thereby cultivating a spiritual or divine personality within us creates balance and gives happiness to the self and others.

Type 5 Spiritual and Divine Personality - Quiet and Expressive, Caring and Letting Go Personality:

Quiet and Expressive:

Their personality is balanced knowing when to be quiet and when to be expressive.

They mold themselves according to the situation. They become quiet and act from the space of experience and maturity. They observe things, people and make decisions wisely. They keep the veins of their horses(self-control) slow and steady.

They don't jump to conclusions. They deal the situation step by step in a genuine manner. They are always calm at the heat of the moment (sign of maturity) exhibiting qualities of patience and tolerance.

Example: They will be calm and quiet when dealing with an angry boss.

Expressive:

They communicate and express their opinion when necessary in a sweet and firm manner. They know when to draw a line and convey their opinions and limits. They know when to take an initiative and stand up. They keep people around them safe and comfortable by being kind and friendly. At the same moment, they provide people their own space and accommodate their weaknesses. They do not judge people based on their weaknesses and take it personally.

Example: They will express their concern and situation to the boss when he has cooled down and behave kindly to him without judging his/her boss based on his anger or gossip about him/her behind their back.

Caring and Letting Go:
They are kind, helpful, generous and available for others. They extend their hand of cooperation when needed without asking for it. They do all actions without expecting any results or appreciation from others. Because of this attitude, they are able to be in a good mood always and give rather than take.

When troubled by others, they are able to let go of negative moments and appreciate the difference of opinion. They do not take anything personally and stay free from all negativity due to their high self-esteem and compassion for others. They understand the value of inner work where the relationship of the self is established and are sustained daily through self reflection and meditation.

Reflection:
 1. What type of personality you think you are from the above personality types?
2. Write the positive and negative aspects of your personality.
3. Choose two people who are closer to you and detect their personality. Write their positive and negative aspects.

Om shanti (I am peace)

The Way of Treating People

In the movie "Dumbo" in a moving train the mother elephant with her friends awaits anxiously for her baby. Shortly the stork delivers the baby elephant in a cloth bundle to the mother elephant. The baby elephant is named Jumbo before he is opened from the cloth bundle with a happy birthday song.

When the mom elephant happily opens the bundle which had a beautiful baby elephant with blue eyes, all her elephant friends adore the baby and call the baby with sweet names.

Baby elephant smiles and becomes proud and happy. In few moments, the baby elephant sneezes and his large ears open up. Seeing those large ears, all the elephant friends immediately tease the baby and make fun out of the baby Jumbo. They even change his name into Dumbo. Hearing this reaction, the baby elephant frowns and becomes sad.

At this point, the mother elephant takes the baby elephant under her wing and shows her temper to the elephant friends. The friends comment about her temper and justify their dislike of the large ears that they were right about the large ears.

Later the mother elephant embraces the baby elephant and when the baby elephant's large ears touch her eyes she gently wraps those large ears around the baby elephant and cuddles him.

Well, having said the story we can observe how people treat each other in this world.

Human beings treat other human beings in the same way as in the story. Like the baby elephant, each human being has inner beauty and goodness along with some weakness like the large ears. When a person exhibits their goodness, everyone:

- adores them
- loves them
- respects them
- wants to be with them

Whereas when the same person exhibits some weakness in a situation (like a sneeze/disturbance), everyone:

- teases them
- ignores them
- makes fun out of them
- blames them
- gives them hard time
- disrespects them
- criticizes them
- gossips behind their back

A person can exhibit goodness and weakness according to their personality and the situations of the life. Everyone does it but the treatment we give to people when they are in their negative space has to be taken care of.

Every human being needs to be,

- Accepted along with their goodness and weakness (blue eyes and large ears).

  > Instead we resist, dislike and hate.

- Accommodated during their mistakes, errors and negative emotions.

  > Instead we judge and punish.

- Tolerated in their anger, fear and stress.

  > Instead we quarrel, get upset and avoid them.

- Believed when they lose hope.

  > Instead we get disappointed, ignore and blame.

- Trusted when they are vulnerable.

  > Instead we complain and wail.

- Told how special they are.

  > Instead we gossip behind their back and find fault with them.

- Appreciated for their hard work and good heart.

  > Instead we get jealous and hesitate cooperation.

- Supported for their initiative, leadership and sharing.

  > Instead we feel we are bossed around due to low self-respect.

- Encouraged when they are trying to transform.

  > Instead we push them down and just don't give

them a second chance.

We give a negative reaction because,
- we get hurt by their negative behavior
- we expect them to behave in a certain way
- of our own ego, fear and insecurity
- of our own lack of discernment of other's needs
- of a lack of communication of our needs

Things don't work out between people because of,
- assumptions — I tend to believe that what I think is right and others are not right as I am. I get caught up in my own understanding that I do not even verify my assumptions with others
- not conveying your feelings then and there (feedback in a loving way) — it's quite important to convey matters to people without putting them in a defensive mode
- misunderstanding — It is all right to misunderstand but sufficient time and effort is required to get clarification
- not being able to let go and forgive
- not being able to see one's own weakness and focusing on others' mistakes and problems

I give permission from my heart to let people be however they are.

I do not endorse it but I am not going to get disturbed by their weakness either!

I take whatever is good in everyone and allow other aspects to sail away from me. The overall spiritual practice is to really focus on our own self and keep an open generous attitude towards others' needs and weaknesses.

I accept (not agree) that people,
- can wear false masks
- can be mean to me
- can be dishonest
- can gossip
- can ignore and insult me
- can betray me

Basically I offer them the space to be however negative they can get to be. But I remember they are just like the baby elephant's large ears. I practice to focus on their goodness(baby elephant's blue eyes). In the above story, the mother elephant wraps the large ears of the baby elephant around it, similarly when people show their negativity I need to find a way to make it positive out of love and understanding.

Some of the below points can help us do that,
- No one is perfect in this world including the saints, psychologists, philanthropists, spiritual teachers.

- Everyone is doing their best in their own scope and area.

- Life is a platform of consistent learning and enjoying the process.

- There is inner beauty in each being on this earth.

- Let my heart be pure and generous.

- Let me lower my expectations of others and be compassionate.

- Let me think of others' pain and suffering before mine.

- Let me imagine other person's situation.

- Truth always wins and it's never proven.

- Not everything can be understood instantly, so let me be patient with myself and others.

The mother elephant in the story can be God and the people who love us dearly who are there for us no matter how we are and what we do. Each one of us always have that unconditional love and acceptance by God.

Reflection:
1.   How do I treat people? Do I discriminate them based on their weaknesses and habits I don't like?
2.   Today can I look their specialities and change my attitude towards them?

Om shanti (I am peace)

Understanding Expectations

We all have expectations of others. An expectation rises from a space of wanting people to be responsible and to fulfill their duties.

Example: A security guard is expected to ensure safety.

Responsibility is expected from others.
So is it all right to have expectations?
In one way yes because expectations rise from the space of responsibility. We feel one is responsible therefore we expect.

Example: A customer care personnel has a responsibility to help his customers. This is what we expect from him.

When that responsibility is not fulfilled, we get upset.
To have expectations are okay but to feel bad when it's not met is what has to be taken care of.

Over Expectation:
When an expectation exceeds a limit and when it gets mixed with our own desire then it becomes over expectation and stress to others. Expectations also arise due to one's needs and desires. People feel pressured to fulfill our needs. Then one person becomes burdened in satisfying the expectation and the other keeps on expecting thereby leaving no happiness and harmony in relationships.

Example: A student has the responsibility to study. But if we expect the student to study continuously and get always top grades is over expectation.

People may feel no matter how much they do the other person is not happy and only complains.

Dissolving Expectations:
Each one has responsibility but along with it they have their own capacity.

Responsibility is same but capacities are different.

Example: A doctor has the responsibility to cure but each doctor is specialized in something. Their capacities to cure vary. To expect every doctor to offer instant cure and getting frustrated is our problem. It is that desire to get cured quickly that creates the expectation.

Desire is to wish more than what is possible. People are aware of the capacity but still wish.

Example: A father knows his daughter's interest is in engineering but still wishes that she would study medicine.

Gradually desires become expectations then upgrade to demands. In a work environment, a boss might have the desire to meet the target on a certain date and thereby increase his expectations of the team which gradually transforms into demands. With demands people stress out.

Stress is common in our daily lives due to desires. People feel stressed for the desire to earn more in order to,

- buy more
- feel richer
- just maintaining a good image among friends or society
- fulfill the wants of family

Reflection:
1.   Do I have demands from someone or a situation?
2.   What is the reason behind it? Is there any desire that is pushing it?
3.   Do I have over expectations?
4.   Do I get upset when my least expectations are not met? Can I teach myself to accept that moment?
5.   Can I understand my responsibility?

With these questions, I can clearly understand what are my desires, expectations and responsibilities of the self. I can transform my attitude for a peaceful life.

Om shanti (I am peace)

Going Beyond Expectations

Expectations are deeply connected with the following:

- Responsibility/Duty/Purpose
- Needs and Wants
- Capacity
- Benchmarks
- Mindsets/Versions
- Perception/Attitude

Expectations and Responsibility:
Expectations are created from duties, purpose and responsibilities of an individual or object. It's like a giver and taker. Responsibility is the giver and expectation is the taker. The problem is that either are not always balanced. The scales keep wavering in our lives.
Example: A new phone is responsible to offer certain features as advertised. It's expected to perform them.

When you call customer care, you expect a certain level of service. The offering of that service is the responsibility of the customer care. A company's or person's reputation is built when they fulfill their responsibilities accurately and they fulfill all the expectations. The problem arises when there are different versions.

My version of responsibility is different from your version of expectation.

Whenever an expectation is not fulfilled, it leads to disappointment, frustration, unhappiness, peace-less, anxiety and stress.

Expectations and Capacity:
Each one delivers their expectation or duty based on their capacity.
Example: I am expected to cook six dishes for lunch but I am capable of doing only three. I am expected to finish the task by 2:00 pm but I can finish it only by 8:00 pm.

Not everyone has the same capacity. When I understand this and operate with people according to their capacity, I can be less disappointed. When I do not understand each one's ability and capacity, I create false expectation towards them and feel frustrated when they do not keep up with it.

Expectations and Perception:
I need to change the perception "Everyone has to fulfill their duty sincerely on time."
Examples:
- I go to a bus station and expect the bus to arrive on time.
- I organize a party and expect everyone to come on time.

Of course performing all tasks on time builds quality and accuracy but not everyone can offer it. I need to prepare myself for both high and low quality, punctuality and delay, accuracy and procrastination.

People are different and each one has their own style.

Basically if I could let go of 'black and white' perception and create an open inclusive attitude then I can be peaceful in my life.

Expectations and Mindsets/Versions:
Each of us develops our own mindset based on our childhood, life experiences and our personality.
Example: For one person, a good teacher is someone who is kind and understanding.

For another person, a good teacher is someone who is strict and disciplined. Here we find 2 versions of a teacher. Each version is true from their experience and belief. They are called versions and mindsets that each individual carries and use it to develop expectations in their life.

Thereby I need to accept that there are different versions of roles, responsibilities, duties and tasks. I cannot fulfill everything nor I can expect my coffee to be perfect.

Example: Milk and sugar sachets are given to make tea/coffee to my own preference. In life too I can tune my expectations accordingly in every situation.

I take happily whatever I receive, then add the required milk/ sugar sachets to whatever is missing in my delivery.

Can I do this?

Instead of blaming and complaining of what I didn't receive and what I was not offered, I can fix things and move on.

Do you feel sometime "But, I deserve it?":
When I paid for the service, when I invested a lot of time and feelings into it, and things don't go the way I expected, I feel irritated and betrayed. I feel failure and sadness.
Let me understand the bigger picture in certain situations. Not everything in life is an equal scale match. "I gave this much, I got this much."

Example: I gave 50, I am supposed to receive 50.

Sometimes I may not receive 50, I may receive only 30. Can I adjust? Adapt? Accept? We always impulse to tie a bell on that cat? Someone has to be blamed! Let the cat roam without a bell. Why do we always want to clearly blame something?

Let me accept the uncertainty.
Let me accept that not everything has to be sorted out.
This will ease my mentality of feeling, "I deserve it."
If you really deserve it, it will find a way to reach you.

The Habit of Raising Someone's Expectation:
The classic example for this is a sales person. They create an aura of this faultless amazing product for you in your mind. Carried away by the poetry and some true facts, you buy the product, then the coming months...you know what happens! Sometimes we tend to increase the expectations of others by mere praise, false promotion and marketing speeches.

So let me be aware in not using above method as I distort the other person's ability to judge and bias them. Let things be natural.

The Habit of Raising Your Expectations:
Some of us have this familiar habit of getting over excited and thrilled. When the reality kicks in, I feel like soda water as the reality is too far away from my imagination.

Example: Your expectations after watching a movie trailer versus watching the full movie after its release.

Any time I raise the bar of expectation, there is a higher chances of disappointment. Playing Cool is the new trend. Being cool with whatever happens is a nice way of living; not too many expectations. Let me not always carry a measuring scale in monitoring the behavior of others and life.

Don't you feel exhausted when you are a perfectionist? Exhaustion happens as there is constant analysis, benchmarking, comparisons, disappointments with created expectations. I would not say don't have any expectations. Let your expectations be realistic, cool and flexible so you are ready to adapt to either Sahara desert or Amazon rainforest.

Reflection:
1. What are some situations where I felt: "I deserve it"? Can I change my perception now for the same situation?
2. Work out lowering your scale on two situations where you have high expectations.

Om shanti(I am peace)

Do You Justify Your Emotions?

All of us tend to justify the way we feel about something. When someone asks you "Why is this upsetting?", you immediately give an explanation as to why you are right to feel that way. You say, "I am angry" because this one behaved in a way that upsets you. You give logic for your anger. You justify "Logically I am supposed to get angry here."

Each time you feel any negative emotion, what does your head say to you?
- You should feel upset now.
- You should get mad with this now.
- You have the right to ignore them.
- You can't keep quiet now, you have to yell!
- They did this, so you are allowed to feel miserable.
- You are going to attend an interview, so you are supposed to feel nervous and scared.

Internally I convince myself that I have a right to feel a negative emotion because of so and so reason. I justify it. I make it seem like I am bound to get emotional.

I have to be afraid/sad/insecure/frustrated otherwise I think that something is wrong with me. There is logic and reasoning for my every negative emotion.

And I can't question that logic. I feel helpless and continue to suffer the emotion because I feel I have no choice.

Example: Someone cheated you. You feel sad about the whole drama. When questioned, you say: "What else I can do about it?"

You allow your being to feel heart-broken and get distressed. Internally you feel this is what I am supposed to feel in this circumstance.

Example:

Your inner programming is:

- When I am being loved, I am supposed to feel that love and happiness.

- When I am being betrayed, I am supposed to feel stupid, sad and heartbroken.

- It is as if all of us have this strong wiring inside us. We can't just shake it off no matter how much we tell ourselves consciously.

How can you rewire yourself?

Recognize your inner logic.

Write some of the incidents where:

- You are supposed to feel that way(negative emotion).
- Those negative emotions just came out of control.
- You felt pressured to feel that negative emotion.
- Identify the inner thoughts that led you to that negative emotion.

Example: I felt sad after I heard someone talking behind my back. I felt pressured to feel sad as I felt I was the victim.

Your inner thoughts could be "I didn't expect this from that person," "I want people around me to love and respect me always."

Understanding the Logic:
The next step is to understand how did you create that negative logic.

- Trace a childhood memory that led you to create that logic.
- Was it any strong past experience related to that logic?
- Ask yourself: "What Am I getting from that logic?", "Why am I so attached to that logic?"

It's all right if you couldn't locate the exact design of your logic.

Example: Logic is "I want the other person to listen to me" and the answer could be "I feel good and respect when someone listens to me."

Let Go of the Logic and Rewiring:
First of all, I should make a conscious decision that I want to be free from all my negative logic that pushes me to negative emotions. I should be willing to do this in the first place. After finishing the steps of identifying and understanding my inner logic, I am preparing myself to let go of it.

Why should I let go?
Because I understand I will lose my peace of mind and happiness because of these negative logic programming inside my head.

Ask yourself:
- Do I like to feel happy?
- Do I want peace of mind?
- Do I like to keep my cool?

If I answer yes to the above questions, then I am ready to begin the process of rewiring.

The Process of Letting Go and Rewiring:
I am going to let go of this right to feel angry; the pressure of feeling a certain way. So I am going to rewire the inner belief/ logic that urges me.

Let me self-talk the following in my meditation,
- Acknowledge the inner logic.
- Change the mindset.
- Let me think positive in this situation.
- What Am I learning here?
- Nothing is a big deal...I can handle it!
- Each one is doing their best.
- I am no one to judge others, the Universal Law of Karma will take care of everything.
- Let me not absorb the hurt and injustice outside of me. Even though they give it to me, it's my choice to take it or not. Let me take care of my inner being first. Let me protect myself.
- At any given point, I am responsible for my thoughts, feelings, decisions and actions. Let me be responsible for peace in my life. Let me not give that control to others. Let me not blame and make myself suffer.
- Let me accept and forgive people's mistakes. Let me master my mind with these positive beliefs and thought patterns.

- I have the right to feel happy, joyful, content and blessed all the time instead of anger, fear, and sadness. Let me choose!

Reflection:
1. Write couple of justifications you offer when confronted a mistake?
2. What is your inner logic in relationships? What are your wired beliefs?

Om shanti (I am peace)

The Habit of Taking Sorrow

In the Brahma Kumaris teachings, there is a slogan "Don't give sorrow nor take sorrow!"

We do our best not to give sorrow but we do easily pickup sorrow. A type of sensitivity within makes us pick up negativity quickly. We do not consciously realize how we hurt ourselves.

Example: You take care of someone who is needy and you give your best with good intentions but you end up getting hurt when that person doesn't appreciate you.

There are many ways one takes sorrow. You can notice your favorite ways of getting hurt and feeling bad. There is a spiritual jargon called "Feeling-proof" which is a state where one doesn't get hurt no matter what happens.

How does one pickup sorrow?
There is no conscious process to feel bad. It just happens. All of a sudden someone's behavior irritates you. In general, most of the sorrow caused by people around us is unintentional. In certain occasions, it can be deliberate.

Example: A person walks into a waiting area, looks at you and sits somewhere away from you.

You can get easily offended by this simple action. That person could have looked at something behind you or just for their convenience could choose a seat away from you. But you get hurt or run a series of waste thoughts because of your habit of easily getting hurt.

Going Beyond the Habit of Taking Sorrow:
Live in Your Own Power:
One of the reasons is low self-respect. When you do not value yourself enough, you easily feel disrespected or insulted. When you have a hundred percent faith in yourself, you do not seek approval from others. There are fewer expectations from your outside world since your inner light guides you; nourishes you. You live in your own power. You become thick skinned.

From Sensitivity towards Sensibility:
Taking sorrow is a sign of sensitivity. Sensibility is to be aware and take things in the right benevolent sense. Approaching problems as opportunities is an act of sensibility. Sensible people are aware of obstacles but they do not blow them up or make them a big deal. Taking sorrow is making small matters big or sometimes even to create non-existent issues.
Example: You can assume your friend is angry with you, so you create distance and live in your own imaginary world of sorrow.

High Expectations, Assumptions and Resistance:
- High expectations cause sorrow.
- Assumptions cause sorrow.
- Resistance causes sorrow.

Ask yourself how many assumptions you make daily about people and situations. Our beliefs, perceptions and past experiences push us to assume most often.

Assumptions can be handled through openness and communication. Being open is to just wait and look. I need to be aware that I don't jump to conclusions and make quick judgments. Things always reveal themselves. Developing patience helps a lot. The moment you judge, you order your heart to feel something because the inner mechanism has processed the outside world and given you a command to feel bad as a result.

When you are open, the feelings are held and unnecessary anxiety, stress, tension, worry is avoided. We resist due to dislikes, desires, preferences and comfort zones. Whenever we resist, we take sorrow from the person or situation.
Example: Internally when you resist a person's idea or opinion, you feel sad or unworthy due to resistance. It is not the person's idea but your resistance causing you sorrow.

We are all habitual in playing the blame game with an illusion that there is always someone or something causing me sorrow.

The truth is our feelings are in our hands and we can choose what to feel at each moment of our lives.

Let us instill a healthy practice: " I will not unnecessarily pickup sorrow from anyone"

- Let things emerge...
- Let people be...
- Let's observe and be patient...
- Let's understand people have their own reasons for everything...

Reflection:

1. What are some of the wrong assumptions I have made in life?
2. When I find myself resisting, can I pause and see where it is coming from?
3. In which situations do I easily take sorrow? Write two of them.

Om Shanti (I am peace)

The Habit Of Making Others Feel Bad

Have you felt that sometimes people make you feel bad? They want you to feel guilty, make you apologize, make you feel that you are a bad person. They become content in doing that to you as that makes them feel good.

Some may do this to you without even realizing it themselves as they are so caught up with the drama of why, what and how. They just need to pin it on somebody. The following are some of the behaviors of the people who have the habit of making others feel bad;

- putting others down
- taunting indirectly
- unnecessary speculation of a situation
- indirect behaviors like that look of avoidance
- sarcastic comments
- trying to plot out who is right and who is wrong
- relating all the past experiences with the current one
- labeling you
- not letting you out of the situation; mentally holding you there
- giving no room for apology or starting over

Why someone makes the other to feel bad?
Ego is the "I am right" feeling. To control others is a hidden expression of "I am above you"and it means to hold an upper hand over others.

Example: At a workplace, the boss might start advising or take over the conversation from the table to show that he holds a higher position than others. He is doing that as he doesn't want to be seen as "bad" or "wrong" or "irresponsible."

He tries to cover up the situation by discussing the weaknesses of others, that way the focus is turned from him to others or the project. It's an aspect of your ego. Ego doesn't want you to feel low (in cases of inferiority complex, it doesn't allow you to feel great). Ego doesn't want you to feel bad and wrong.

So the habit of making others feel bad is a defensive mechanism from your ego. If there is not enough power in the self, there is always blame and finger pointing at others. When someone is exhibiting with this habit, it's the ego of the person which is making them behave like that. They might even feel that they are in fact doing justice in saying who is right and who is wrong.

The Behaviors of People who makes Others Feel Bad: Response through Words - Keeping you on the hook: Whenever any mistake happens, they like to keep you in that guilt mode and they don't like letting go either by you or them. It is a difficult emotional phase because no matter what you do, they want to be caged and try to keep you caged too. **Example:** Say you forgot to do a task given by this person (the one who has the habit of making others feel bad). You realized it and apologized. But this person will not leave you just like that. They will give explanations round and round to make you feel bad. Your face changes and your feelings go a little bit deeper. You apologize again saying: "I am sorry it caused you so much distress." Still nothing changes. They do not let you go off the hook that easily.

You stand there getting extremely puzzled, becoming slightly emotional and slowly entering into your guilty mode. You feel guilty. Still it's not over yet. Comments are made and your past is dug up and related numerous times to the current situation. You are in a place of collapse and emotionally furious to get out of the situation (cut the call or leave the spot). None of your apology or explanation matters. Finally you are convinced of this awful feeling of "I am bad."

Silent Response:
Based on the personality of the person who has the habit of making others feel bad, their behavior pattern changes. In this case, when facing any unpleasant situation they play quiet in passive aggressive mode.

The effect turns out to be the same for the victim in fact more frustrating than the previous behavior. There is no way of getting out and you are stuck living with that situation. The method the person uses here to make others feel bad is by avoiding them and silently making them feel unworthy.
Example: Avoid sitting with you while having meals at home, Cold behaviors.
Whenever you feel or say: "They deserve this" or "They deserve only this much" then you have the habit of making others feel bad.

The whole idea of making others feel bad is about who is right and who is wrong then you are stuck in this ideology that you forget to be compassionate. The idea of justice is caught up in the head and the door of the heart closes.

Do you have this habit?
Whenever you hear people telling you "Don't make me feel bad" then take a pause and check what you did that they make this comment. Without justifying yourself, sincerely search for any flaws in your behavior. Sometimes we find our intentions are good but behavior is hurtful.

How to handle a person who has this habit?
- Understanding that they are acting from the space of ego and it is their habit.
- Staying in your self-respect; knowing who you are.
- Ability to let go.
- Forgive and forget.
- Practicing a level of tolerance and not allowing things to take control over you.

We do get affected when others give us a hard time either through silent treatment or speaking to make us feel bad. But if I recognize this is an illusion of right and wrong, good and bad, I can move on.

Everyone is doing their best and performing their script in life. I pretty much have no control over any one's script except mine.

If people are causing me distress, it's just their script. My script is to accept, understand, let go, tolerate little bit, communicate, forgive and keep myself peaceful and happy.

How to transform if you have this habit?

I sit with myself and reflect on the effect of my behavior upon others. The Karma I create by hurting others. I hurt others because I am hurt. In contemplation and meditation, one can take care of one's feelings, give peace to them, understand its roots and heal the emotions.

I develop the ability to understand that it is my responsibility to treat others well no matter what others do to me. When I take care of myself by being compassionate, tolerant, sweet, merciful, respectful and loving, then this habit will die on its own.

All negative habits arise from the emptiness of positivity. I use the habit of making others feel bad to make myself feel good about myself. When I begin to stay in my self-respect, then my heart will have the capacity to let others be what they want to be.

Also, the majority of people immediately realize the mistake once they make one, therefore I do not have to emphasize it to make them feel bad. Rather,

- Let me be compassionate and offer co-operation.
- Let me console them and be easy.
- Let me make others comfortable.
- Let me not expect perfection.
- Learn to live with flaws and imperfections.

- Give room for other's mistakes.

Practice:
- I am a compassionate being.
- I allow everyone to play their script.
- I focus on improving my script only.

Om shanti (I am peace)

The Habit of Gossiping

There is an inner aggression in the mind. There is this pressure built up about the person or situation, all the waste thoughts " I did this, they did that","This happened and that shouldn't have happened","It was a complete injustice","It is ridiculous".

I need to let the pressure out, I can't hold the juicy reports I learned about someone whom I may or may not know. I need to share it to someone. To release this aggression I seek my listener. I reach out to my gossip circle and vent it out. Then one by one, I meticulously repeat the story and enjoy the speculation.

It is as though gossip gives me a wicked joy. I need to clear the system, download my judgments, feelings and comments to someone. Without it, I cannot sleep!

Why do we gossip?
Because:
- I do not have the courage to talk about that person directly.
- I am not in a position to confront them, e.g., boss.
- I am not directly involved but still will like to talk about their life, e.g., movie actors.
- It is a venting process to download the thoughts of my mind to others.

- It is a way to feel better when compared to others's problems.
- To vent out jealousy and envy.
- To kill time.
- To divert the attention from the self.
- To belong and relate to a group.
- I love to create false stories.
- I blow up matters out of proportion and context.

What are the consequences of gossip for others?

When I gossip,

- It is not necessarily the truth; so I may be spreading falsehood.
- My attitude towards the gossiped person changes.
- I also make others change their opinion about the gossiped person.
- Indirectly I am hurting the gossiped person.
- I spread negativity and heaviness in the atmosphere.
- I show a lack of empathy and compassion for the subject.
- In a way, I am a coward to speak about someone behind their back.
- I destroy someone's happiness and morale.
- I demotivate and judge others without knowing the truth.

What are the consequences of gossip for the self?

- I lose my integrity and trust. People who know my gossiping nature will not trust me easily. I may be the last person to know.
- I become a negative person who always focus only on negativity and feed upon the negativity of others.

- I can be easily distracted by others.
- My valuable time and energy is wasted.
- I may be popular in social circles but may have very few true friends.
- I also develop an emotional dependence on the people with whom I share my stories.

Solutions:

1. Change your Conversations into Positive:

Instead of spending time in gossiping about others, you can have positive conversations. You can share the same news and reports in a positive limelight and outlook. Instead of commenting, criticizing and judging you can appreciate and talk well about the person.

2. Don't Avoid but Reduce your Gossip Time:

Sometimes my social circle can gossip, but instead of avoiding them, I can be passive and reduce my exposure time in those matters. If possible, I can steer the conversation into positive and fun matters.

3. Invest your Time in Beneficial Things:

Time is an invaluable treasure. Do not waste your time in hurting others. Invest your time and energy in projects and activities that brings benefit to the self, others and the community.

4. Focus on the Self:

When you are focused on the self rather on others, the habit of gossip finishes.

Create goals and work on achieving them. Be an example and inspire others.

5. Power to Accommodate:
A good leader is someone who merges the mistakes of others and has good wishes. Co-operate and help people in their difficulties instead of becoming their enemy. You can win many hearts.
Let me share people's specialties, qualities and good actions to my best ability. I create a healthy, positive and harmonious atmosphere wherever I go.

Reflection:
1. Do you gossip? Are you mindful of the words that come out of your mouth?
2. How do you feel when you are the subject of gossip?
3. Change your next gossip session into a positive conversation. Write the results.

Om shanti (I am peace)

Handling Complaining Hearts

Have you wondered how do I ever satisfy this person? When will they become happy or content with me?

There are complaining hearts around us. They constantly blame, criticize, mock, taunt and complain about us like non-stop radios. Do you get tired and frustrated with such characters?

Complaining Hearts make us feel unworthy, uncomfortable and at times awful. They spread an atmosphere of discontentment and most of them are grumpy and some of them are silently grumpy. They might fall into the category of perfectionism and egotism.

Living with Complaining Hearts:
No matter what you do and how well you do, they are amazing fault finders. Even if the best soup is offered to them, there is always something to complain about. Here you are feeling good having made a delicious soup; but when your delighted heart faces a word of criticism and the dissatisfactory body language of complaints, your little heart loses its happiness almost instantly.

You enter into a state of commotion, justification and 1000 questions arise with 10,000 answers to it. You absorb their complaining image, vibrations and lose yourself into it.

Why Complaining Hearts Complain? What happens inside them?

There are various reasons for complaining hearts to complain. Not everyone falls under the same category.

Complaining Hearts Type 1:

Some hearts are basically discontented; in other words they are souls who have developed the habit of staying dissatisfied, unhappy and discontent perhaps since their childhood. It is a kind of nature some souls easily dwell in.

How to handle: When we understand it's their habit or nature, we can reduce our dependency on their feedback towards us because we know it is not us; it is just their perception. Whatever they complain about is not genuine.

Complaining Hearts Type 2:

Ego is the reason for certain hearts to complain. As they think too high about themselves and perfect, they tend to find faults with others' activities. It is too painful for them to digest that you are right or better than them. They express their ego through complaints by putting you down and making you doubt yourself.

How to handle: As these hearts make you feel unworthy, it is very important to maintain your self-dignity in their presence. Maintaining your creative heart and listening to their feedback without taking it personally can save you.

Complaining Hearts Type 3:
Perfectionism is the reason for these hearts to complain because they want everyone and everything to be perfect (in their opinion).

So they try to tune, fix, alter others towards perfection in their eyes. They want to make you perfect just the way they like. They bombard you constantly with their ideas, advices and corrections.

How to handle: As being with such hearts makes you tired, always remember your uniqueness and inner beauty.

How to protect yourself?
Listen to them with peace at that moment and later on just do your best in your style. There is no point in arguing with such hearts. You will never be listened.

Acceptance of every flaw and weakness in this world is real humanity and spirituality.

It's not that complaining hearts are bad or good. There is no right or wrong, it is just their weakness. But I need to learn what goes inside them irrespective of their action and motive. I need to protect my feelings and stop myself from being hurt by the complaining hearts. I am affected because I give importance to other's words than mine. When I trust myself, I can be comfortable in my element. To complain is their choice and to keep doing my best is my freedom.

I need not thrive to make them content; as they will never be. But neither do I isolate them or react to them. I make an effort to understand them and teach my heart to stay beyond the influence of their complaints.

I also check sincerely for any feedback or truth in their complaints. I change myself humbly if there is any. Gradually I will be all right in their company and play my role gracefully without getting disturbed.

My behavior may or may not cause a slight impact on the complaining hearts but I will be free from the fear and frustration of hearing complaints. My heart will be full and content knowing my true value. My vibrations of contentment will automatically provide safety, peace and contentment to other hearts.

Reflection:
1. Do I complain about others?
2. Do I get upset when others complain about me? Can I see the truth and go beyond?

Om Shanti (I am peace)

Patience Vs Positive Confrontation

It is a tough decision to make whether to stay patient for another second or to just go ahead and confront it. Just one moment of wrong discernment causes repentance.

Example: In a business meeting or family gathering, one should know when to listen patiently and when to present a fact/solution.

Understanding Patience and Positive Confrontation:
Being Patient:
It is the life's biggest lesson that everyone learns as they move along. Patience is a beautiful quality that serves the owner with its precious gifts. One who is patient receives the best and moves along the journey without getting hurt. Patient ones are wise and mature. Their hearts are strong and big to absorb and withstand anyone and anything. One is patient from inner wisdom and life's experiences.

When is patience visible?
1. Patience is exercised while listening.
2. When something is happening beyond your control.
3. When someone is operating from their space of weakness, e.g., anger, stress, irritation, frustration, lazy, criticize, blame.
4. Patience with someone's inability, e.g., physically challenged, aged, kids, diseased, drug addicts, mentally ill.
5. Patience with nature like weather, natural disasters and calamities.

Positive Confrontation:

The ability to,

1. Take initiative
2. Speak up
3. Take effort or action
4. Communicate an idea, opinion or a thought
5. Express one's feelings and emotions
6. Stand up for justice
7. Save life
8. Voice for others

Positive Confrontation is an art not everyone practices. Special ones depict the art of positive confrontation but all can develop it. One who confronts is like a leader or savior. They are the go-getter type. They believe in "Do or Die" principle. They are determined, bold and courageous. Their hearts thrive for a positive outcome, justice and righteous action.

They speak-up and take an action at the right moment. They grab the opportunity for the best interests of the family/work/society.

The Divine Balance of Patience and Positive Confrontation:

To be patient and to confront is a balancing art.

We can be patient and at the same time we need to know when to positively confront.

Situation 1: Dealing with an Angry person

When the angry person is exhibiting his/her anger, I am patient understanding the heat of the situation and the person's personality, position, relationship and weakness. Once the other has downloaded their emotions enough, I positively confront with clarity, sweetness and courage. I patiently explain the figures and facts without expecting them to accept and understand me immediately. Once I confront, I let go and become string free of the other person.

When I exercise this balance of patience and positive confrontation, I can be emotionally free and have a cool mind and stable intellect.

Situation 2: Dealing One's Weakness

Whenever I get stressful, anxious, nervous, angry, depressed or afraid of any emotion, I become patient with my own being. In other words, whatever I think, speak or act in my space of weakness, I do not judge myself.

I patiently allow myself to pass the dark space I am in. Any weakness is not permanent. They are passing clouds. They will eventually pass.

The healthy way to handle a negative emotion is to be patient with it at its moment of occurrence in my mind. When I constantly judge myself, it takes me into a further dark space deep down and I lose the power, energy or even hope to resolve! Thereby being patient with myself is a loving way of nurturing my being.

Once these emotions are settled down, I positively confront myself. I become detached from my weakness as if my pure space is different from my bad space. I relate myself with the pure space and reflect on my weaknesses to transform. Like a mother, I listen to my mind's hurts, stories and with my wisdom and experience, I console and teach myself. I need to positively confront my dark space (weaknesses) if I would like to transform.

Being patient with myself enables me to love and respect my weaknesses and strengths as a whole inner being. I am in the pathway to restore my inner peace and happiness; where without patience I cannot continue walking my pathway!

Reflection:
1. Write one situation where you were patient instead of confronting others? What didn't allow you to positively confront the situation?
2. How much is your percentage of patience? Do you only impatiently confront everything? Write two practices that will allow you to be more patient.

Om Shanti (I am peace)

Everyone and Everything needs Space

There is work space, home space, storage space, parking space and different types of spaces. We allocate space for physical materials and tasks in our life.

But do we give space for a person? In other words do I give space for another person's thoughts, feelings, ideas, opinions and wishes? Do I allow them to be who they are?

Each one of us has a script to play. Good or bad, we all have a script. Each script is unique and the whole life around me has a script too.

When I tend to interfere or get annoyed by someone's script then I am not giving them their space to play their script.

Script covers one's habits, personality traits, recorded patterns, ideas, opinions, nature, behavior, attitude and belief system.
Example: A carpenter needs his space to create something with the logs of wood and tools. If he is not given his space, he will still work but his work will not be efficient.

Giving Space for One's Task:
Say you have to bake a cake. You found your recipe and you are work in progress mode. Your script is set on baking now. But if people around you are constantly commenting on the

way you bake, giving you corrections and ideas, will you be able to finish your baking?

No, and even if you do so, you would feel that you didn't get your space to work and next time you make sure that there is no one in the house when you bake the cake. We expect personal space, likewise we should also provide space to others and not interfere/comment/push the other.

Each tree takes its own time to grow. A rose plant might grow quicker than a coconut tree. Likewise one can take longer to finish a task than the other.

I just have given them their space rather than getting annoyed/irritated/upset/pushy/bossy and raising questions.

Giving Space for One's Behavior/Action:
People behave according to their script. Script is the way they play their role. As we see and interact with people, there is a background judgment going on in our heads. This is called interference. I question their script.

I not only question but also get affected and blame the person and their script. The moment I think:
- Why this person is talking like this
- How can he cut me off in the freeway
- Why didn't she smile at me
- How can they treat me like this
- I deserve respect
- I end up always waiting in the bank

- The officers are not efficient
- I helped so much but she didn't even care
- He is so mean
- She is always late

Then I am trying to control the other person's script. I want it to be the right way or the way I wanted it to be. I have to understand that people behave according to their judgment, feelings and their script. I can only change and control my script and not that of others. Rather than raising questions and getting disturbed, I can accept them as they are and tune myself accordingly.

Say I am driving and when I see a stone in my way, I just turn my car in other direction. I do not stop the car and ask, "Why the stone is here? Who put this?" Similarly I work on myself to adjust with the person who is troubling me instead of blaming or becoming a victim. I have the power to create and change. I can make my script to be completely easy, cool, light, accepting and focused.

We live in auto pilot mode, i.e., there is no control of our emotions; they come and go as they wish. Raja Yoga helps us switch to manual mode where you can erase, write, develop and modify your script. Effort and attention is required in manual mode.

I am consciously thinking and creating thoughts, teaching myself good and bad. Once this process is completed, I can put myself in automatic mode to be peaceful, loving and happy always without any effort. I have the power to rewrite my script. Whenever I realize something deeply, I obtain the power to change my script.

I am a master creator!

Reflection:

1. How much control I have over my script?
2. Do I pay attention to my script or I constantly looking at how others are playing theirs?
3. What positive aspects would I like to reprogram in my script?

Om Shanti (I am peace)

The Fear Of People Getting Upset

How many times do you think?
- Oh! I don't want my spouse to get upset with me!
- If I say this, my sister would be really upset with me
- Oh boy, if I miss today's meeting my boss would be very upset with me

All our life, we don't want to upset people around us. Concern and Care is different from worry. We do have to take care of the feelings and emotions of people around us but at the same time we do not need to get caught up with what people's reactions would be for our actions. There is fear of people's reactions.

This fear makes me,
- anxious
- postpone decisions
- avoid/neglect/go around
- extremely worried and bothered
- suppress myself
- uncomfortable
- unmotivated to do anything new
- lose my happiness

So why do I get this fear? What causes it?

Because I am too much concerned about others. When I am doing something beneficial and righteous, then I have to let go of the fear and use my courage to go ahead and do it. I need not bother about people getting upset with me. It is quite all right and they will understand me one day. Eventually they will get my point and pure intention. I do what I have to do.

If I keep holding my decisions or actions until the other person is pleased or approves, I can never be happy and peaceful. I will be stuck and can only describe my misery to others.

Example: I love doing social work on weekends but my friends are upset with me because of my non availability for a party. I can follow my heart and need not worry about people getting upset with me.

I need to set my priorities. Not always, one can explain the reasoning for one's actions. One's pure and good intentions cannot be always understood by another. The other might not find sense in something that you cherish. Giving space to others is essential but if you are not given your space, stop worrying and feeling bad. Go ahead and let time explain everything.

I should also develop a never-mind attitude. It is necessary to free myself from this fear. Fear captures peace! As I have to follow my heart, it doesn't mean I can be arrogant and mean in my behavior. I do have to stay polite, firm and keep my mind undisturbed from these thoughts of people getting upset. I perform action with peace and love.

I understand and know "Yes this is going to upset him/her" but I am going to do it anyway. I am true to myself and I do have to tolerate the consequences:

- troubles
- bad name
- comments
- criticism
- obstacles
- upset faces
- silent treatment

I remind myself that the other person is ignorant of my good intention and they want to control people.

Playing the Game:

Some souls use it as a threat. They know that you will revert or change your mind if they show that they are upset with you.
Example: Say if the wife is upset with her husband's decision and she persists being upset; eventually her husband might change his decision.

Pleasing Others:

I am not here to please anyone. The truth is I cannot please any one all the time. People may not like everything I do or speak. They may become upset or irritated with me but it is not my scope to go and make them feel better.

I can change myself according to others but not to the extent that I lose my spiritual identify or uniqueness.

If my motto is to please someone constantly, hurt is guaranteed. No matter how much I do things in a proper way, people will always still find something to complain about me. So shake it off, maintain focus and keep moving.

Reflection:
1. Whom do you think will get upset with you the most?
2. What happens to you when you are with them?
3. Try to be fearless with that person and do one fearless act a week.

Om shanti(I am peace)

Getting Upset & Blame Game

Some get upset with little things and some with big things. Most of us have the habit of blaming someone when we get upset.

Why we get upset?
When things don't go my way, I get upset.
Who made me upset?
I believe people and situations make me upset.
What do I do when I am upset?
- Blame
- Project

Blame Game:
I play the blame game whenever a mistake happens. My wired response is to find someone to blame. The majority of the times I blame everyone apart from myself.

Why do I play the blame game?
- Because I am afraid to look within and take responsibility for my behavior and mistakes.

- The inner world has so many cobwebs that it's too dark to go within and check out what's happening. It has been ages since I connected with my core.

- I am too scared to sort out my fears and insecurities so I find an escape to blame.

- By blaming others, I take the focus away from me and console myself that: "It's not me, it's them."

Projection:
When I cannot handle the pressure, I pin it and project it on others.
Example: My boss gave me a hard time at work and I project that anger towards my kids at home.

When I cannot react or respond a negative emotion to a person, I project the same negative emotion to,
- people who I take for granted, e.g., family
- people who don't retaliate, e.g., kids
- people who are quiet and passive, e.g., introverts

Taking Responsibility:
It takes a lot of courage to understand that I am upset with my own reaction and not with others.
I am responsible for my thoughts, feelings, emotions, decisions and actions. Only when I take responsibility, I can bring inner change. Until then, I will only be blaming all things external to me.

It is very easy to play the blame game; throw the ball on other's court. Initially it is not a fun process to look within and check my behavior. But, when I reap the fruit of this inner work, all the effort is worth it! I can experience a great self-control, serenity and maturity in my life.

At every situation, instead of looking whose fault was it, let me take responsibility and check what I could have done better. Is there anything I can shift within me to resolve the problem. This attitude will help me to ease all issues instead of just playing the blame game.

When I blame others,
- people get hurt
- they will become defensive
- they will not trust me again
- they will blame me when they get a chance

When I do not blame and take self-responsibility,
- people will respect me
- they will become my friends
- they will support and stand by me
- they will forgive me

Don't Pin-point rather find Solution:
Even though I am upset and there is great damage, in order to create harmony it is better to find solution rather than pointing fingers at each other.

Example: Someone broke my favorite glass vase. The moment I find the vase is broken, what is my first thought and question? "Who broke the vase?". Even before picking up the broken pieces, I need to find out the culprit. My mind doesn't get peace until I find out.

Say if I broke the glass vase, what will be my first thought? It will be: "Let me fix it!" I swiftly move to finding a solution. I may feel guilty but I am not stuck. I readily accept my fault and move on. But I am not able to do it when others do the same mistake?

Power to Accommodate/Adjust/Merge is a beautiful power where the heart sees others' mistakes the same way as they see their own. The ability to accept and treat others with the same love, respect and forgiveness as they do themselves.

Therefore let us stop the habit of blame and develop self-respect to accept our faults and mistakes. Love and cooperation is automatically received because of the honest courageous heart.

Reflection:
1. How often do you blame others?
2. Recall a situation where you blame others and write what could you have done instead by taking responsibility.
3. What are the some of the solutions I can create instead of pin-pointing?

Om Shanti (I am peace)

Understanding Anger

Anger is a disturbance of my feelings expressed loud or passive. Anger is a defensive tool used by many people to accomplish tasks and to protect or prove themselves.

Is Anger necessary?
Do you feel that anger is essential to get things done?
- I am not angry but I am little upset!
- Anger is part of life; it has to be expressed!
- Everyone becomes angry; so what's a big deal?

Since we were kids, we have been seeing a world of anger around us, dad getting mad with mom, mom getting upset with kids, siblings fighting with each other,, neighbors quarreling, friends taunting, adults screaming at each other.

But does this world really need anger?
Do I think this is how things work in this world?
There are various doors in our mind that anger knocks and enters. Some of the doors are:
- Irritation
- Frustration
- Upset
- Dislike
- Aggression

There are four types of anger categorized based on the frequency of one's anger.

Quick Anger or Short tempered:
There are people who get angry for all teeny tiny matters. Their ego gets hurt easily and they become defensive. They hold a low level of tolerance and patience.
Personality: They are grumpy, complaining, rude and basically unhappy with people and life's events around them.
Situations: Every little thing can make them irritated.

Reasonable Anger:
They get angry only when something goes wrong. They react to it as they find a good reason behind their anger. They have justifications and a right reason for their anger. Their tolerance level is of medium level but not much.
Personality: They are peaceful and nice as long as there is no problem in the air.
Situations: arriving late, lazy worker, forgetting to pay the bill, ill treatment by people, favorite objects getting broken.

Occasional Anger:
These souls get angry only for larger damage. They give enough chances and forgive others but still when something is persisting, they blow up. They hold a good amount of tolerance and patience for a long period of time. They only go to the space of anger when their buttons are pushed strongly by a valid occurrence.
Personality: They are peaceful and have cool nature.

Situations: Finding someone repeating mistakes, someone was physically hurt or injured due to carelessness, huge conflicts.

Quiet Anger:
You might have seen some people who have absolutely never gotten angry or even raised their voice in their entire life. They undergo suppression and they are passively aggressive. They might have been brought up in a controlled environment. Due to their passive nature, they might never open up or express their anger due to fear.
Personality: They are calm, sweet and loving but they do hold their anger internally.
Behavior: Silent treatment, avoidance, gossip and revenge.

We all move into these different zones of anger based on our moods and built in personality. Like the flip sides of the coin, in life it is essential to,
1.   Deal your own anger.
2.   Handle angry people.

Anger comes for a reason and there is a message conveyed before it goes outside to attack others.
1.   Identify your zone of anger listed above.
2.   Catch your thoughts in the mind — they are like this:
- I don't like this
- It is wrong!
- How could they do this to me?
- I will teach a lesson to him/her
- They hurt me!

- Why is it happening?
- Why they are not listening/understanding me

If we observe, all the above thoughts are either a judgement or a question. Anger begins with these questions in our minds. As I repeat these questions again and again, I feed fuel to my anger. If these questions are answered and if I become non-judgmental, I can transform my anger into a genuine calm communication language.

3. Look for the hidden messages that is conveyed to me. Whenever things don't go my away and my buttons are pushed, what is the positive message life is giving me? **Example:** "Knock Knock,"maybe I just have to look at their point of view.

Om Shanti (I am peace)

How to Deal with Your Own Anger

One of the effective methods to deal with our own anger is to apply the pause, think and act approach.

Solution 1: Pause, Think and Act
Pause Mode:
An effective way of transforming one's anger is to pause; in other words to delay all responses. Active aggressive people tend to give immediate reactions. They think and act fast. Therefore the first step is to postpone all your replies.

Whenever I find someone's behavior pushing my button and demanding a certain output from me, I can respond to them that I will get back to them in few minutes/hours/days based on the situation. This is the pause mode. I can prevent the disasters of my raging anger towards that person using this mode.

Examples where pause mode can be applied:
- An annoying new email in your inbox
- Conversations or decisions in a relationship
- Your kid asks your approval for something which you don't agree with or are not happy about.
- You are encountering a person who has hurt you earlier
- Situations of handling mistakes and faults of others.

Any situation that is triggering my anger, causing those boiling wavering thoughts inside me, I hold, pause and take a deep breath! Those thoughts are my signal to pause.

I tell myself that I would give them my response after a certain time. Such delayed responses are commonly acceptable. I would at least get a few minutes as a breathing time to ponder upon the situation, my emotions and my decision. Most conflicts occur because of jumping to conclusions, assumptions and impulsive decisions.

Think Mode:
In this mode, I reflect the problem calmly and slowly.
As the time passes, most of the emotions fade away. Still, there are some emotions which occur or increase whenever the situation is recalled.
In this mode, I can take an extra step to;
- Change my attitude
- Mellow my Ego
- Change my view
- Change my negative beliefs
- Employ Patience
- Forgive, and
- Display tolerance

I go into reflection and check if I am using my ego? This reflection space reminds me not to give sorrow to anyone irrespective of the justice I hold.
- I try to change my attitude from blame and attack to a kind and patient one.

- I communicate without getting emotional.
- I change my vision into positive, I try to understand the other person's view and intentions.
- I use my heart rather than my head.
- I loosen my beliefs and intend to adjust.

Action Mode:
When my pause and think mode is successful, my actions will automatically reflect peace and coolness.

There is no hastiness, rather I become an image of maturity and calmness.

- I feel good because I am controlled and I choose my actions consciously.
- I will never feel guilty as I processed my thoughts before I acted.
- I will not be creating any karmic bondage with anyone.
- I will be providing a mature composed response.
- I will be respectful in my interaction.
- I will hold my stand without getting disturbed.

In action mode, since I allow my heart to work in my tasks and interactions, there is peace and harmony.

Solution 2: Change my Belief System
I often become angry whenever things don't go my way.
I get attached to this belief: "Everything should work out according to my desires and needs and when they don't I am supposed to feel sad." We all create various hard core beliefs

right from our childhood. Belief is the strong reason that drives us mad.

Examples of some of our beliefs:

- Everything should be perfect.
- No one should lie to me.
- Everyone should treat me with respect.
- No one should gossip about me.
- My child should listen to me.
- No one should come late to my meeting.

Whenever the above beliefs doesn't get fulfilled, I get upset and angry.

Reflection:

1. How many times was I able to pause today?
2. What did I do in my think mode? Did my mind listen to me?
3. How were my actions after a pause?

Om Shanti (I am peace)

Dealing with Angry People

What not to do:
- Do not judge
- Do not question
- Do not fight
- Do not become a victim
- Do not feel self-pity
- Do not hold any grudge

Rather:
- Accept and listen with calmness.
- Just observe...watch... not react.
- Peel the skin of anger and see the soul that is in distress for justice, love, peace and respect.

An angry person is someone who is adamant, arrogant and yells because of a certain inner need. They feel they can get it by yelling or bossiness.

Example: A parent yelling to a teenager is seeking respect in disguise and a teenager shows his/her rage is seeking acceptance.

When I can see this inner need, I can be merciful in their presence instead of getting annoyed. Then I can be calm and respond rather than reacting and attacking them. I react because my respect or love is threatened by their anger and I become defensive. If I have complete self-love and dignity I would not go to this space and will just observe the game of anger.

Armor of Tolerance:
Tolerance is a beautiful quality. One who has the power of tolerance can never be in sorrow. Like the mother earth tolerates everything done in her lap. Similarly adopt the motherly quality of tolerance in regard to the souls who are angry.

Why should I tolerate? For whose sake Am I tolerating?
I think I am tolerating because of him/her. No, I am tolerating for my own cause. I am protecting my inner peace and sanity of the mind.

Tolerance doesn't mean I am controlled or I allow people to walk over me. Tolerance is used at those moments of confronting angry people's behavior. So I withstand the negative injustice attitude, expressions, feelings, words and actions of the angry people at that very moment.
I do not fall to their level and fight/argue/plead/explain myself; that is being tolerant. I can always communicate and explain to that angry person when they calm down.

Being tolerant is smart as I am aware that the intellect of an angry person doesn't work/analyze/process any information. Tolerance protects me from becoming serious and emotional. Tolerance understands the angry person's treatment towards me is not from the heart.

Tolerance lets me observe and keep myself in truth and not to get carried away by the fire of falsehood.

I do not tolerate by force but by understanding the other person's:

- Capacity
- Weakness
- Character and Personality

Acceptance not Resistance:

Due to our belief system we resist angry behavior. Our belief system is "No one is supposed to be angry," "Everyone should be nice and sweet."

When I change my belief system that anger is a way some people express their needs, then I won't resist that emotion of anger.

I do not agree but just acknowledge the emotion.

I develop acceptance in this way. As long as I resist "Why people become angry? It is bad; they are bad people." I will only be miserable and can never handle them. I will be unable to pacify that soul and transform their anger.

With acceptance, tolerance and patience I can cool down an angry soul in due time. I also need to speak out and communicate my limits. Take actions to defend myself but I do everything without becoming a victim and giving sorrow to myself. To get affected by anger is taking sorrow. Practice BK Teaching: "Neither give sorrow nor take sorrow!"

Reflection:

1. What are your reactions while dealing with angry people?
2. What is your percentage of tolerance? If you tolerate, do you tolerate by force?
3. Practice acceptance for a day and write down your results.

Om Shanti (I am peace)

Passive Aggressive Anger

Passive people express anger in a different manner. It is not visible but noticeable. It can be easily sensed by people around them.

Some of the subtle behaviors of passive anger:

- Expressing anger through body language.
- Rejection.
- Ignoring.
- Silent treatment.
- Gossip.
- Manipulation.
- Backstabbing.
- Criticizing in a polished and clever manner.
- Wearing False Masks.

The passive aggressive ones are at times stubborn in staying silent and trigger others' reactions. No matter how much you persuade or request them, they may not open up and the below are some of their behaviors.

- Staying upset until the other apologizes to me.
- Staying stubborn in silence till the other gives up.
- Making someone guilty by emotionally reminding them about their mistakes in an indirect manner.
  Example: Subtle taunting during conversations

How to Handle a Passive Aggressive Angry Person:
You may get frustrated and lose your patience while dealing
with a passive aggressive person. As they are introverted and
generally not keen in communication, it might be challenging
to know what they are thinking.

We need to understand that it's their nature to be passive like
you are active. Each one has different personalities which are
comfortable for them. You need to build trust and be gentle
with passive ones. Give them time and clarify your intentions
with them. You may not get an immediate response but if you
are sincere, eventually they will let go of their anger.

How to Handle your Own Passive Anger:
As a passive person, I suppress my anger and emotions within.
This habit builds pressure and stress both to the being and the
body. Nothing can ever be completely suppressed, this is why
the anger gets expressed indirectly in various ways. But still,
the pressure is building up and eventually one day it leads to
explosion of all suppressed emotions.

When I suppress, I am not happy either. I am hurt and I walk
around with hurt. I am not ready to positively confront the
person who I had a problem with. I avoid the contact of this
person. I keep ignoring them and escape from dealing with it.

Power to Face:
It is essential to use the power to face. I need to face and
resolve the problem. I need to voice my opinion and

communicate my feelings to the other person. I need not be a silent victim and be bullied by active aggressive people.

Just because I am calm, it doesn't give others the liberty to vent their anger on me!

I need to take the necessary measures to handle my emotions in a healthy manner. I make myself comfortable and confident in having conversations with people especially the negative matters.

Example: If I don't like the way my colleague speaks with me, I need to voice my feedback to him/her in a healthy manner.

Muster the Courage:

I don't have to be a doormat and be exploited by others. I can stand up for myself. I will be bold and courageous. Sometimes, all it takes is "one word" or "one act" of courage. The moment you can take the first step, all the steps follow.

Do not be afraid of what others think or say. Trust and express the self.

Fear is the biggest enemy of a passive aggressive person. Fear suppresses the true potential of a person. Fear is just an illusion of one's mind. Let go of your fears and be transparent with others. Honesty will reward harmony in relationships. I can be direct and honest with people instead of hiding my emotions. When I am honest, I give others a chance to bring about a change.

It does takes time to move from passive aggressiveness to a communicative mode but with baby steps, anything is possible!

Reflection:
1. Are you a passive aggressive person? List some of your passive reactions.
2. Write two of your suppressive emotions. Write behaviors of people you do not agree with.
3. Can you communicate to them in a positive confrontative way? Try it and write the results.

Om shanti (I am peace)

Negative Karma – The Invisible Curtain

The word "Karma" is uttered by almost all of us and the teaching can be found in every scripture of the world. Karma means action. Good Karma means good deeds and Bad Karma is negative action. Good deed is any action that causes benefit to anyone or anything. This applies to a human being/animal/ natural resource (water, electricity) and living forms of nature. Negative Karma is any action causing sorrow to the self or others. It acts like an invisible curtain between two people where one cannot see the other person's true self clearly. They cannot see or pick up the feelings of the person's heart with whom they have negative karma.

Questions of life:
- Do you feel that the other person is not getting your point or understanding your intention? Why don't they understand me?
- No matter how much you do, the other person still hates/ rejects/doesn't forgive you? Why don't they accept me?
- No matter how much you try to please that soul and do good for them, still they consider you as their enemy or keep you at a distance. Why don't they like me?
- Why? Everyone is loved by this person except you!
- Why does this happen only to me? Why Me? Why I am the only person who fails?

The worst part is Why Me always? And many such questions arise continually and they are merged inside unanswered.

"Negative Karma" could be one of the reasons of why things happen to us and only to us.

When there is negative karma between two souls, because of the curtain blockage, they cannot come closer. They cannot harmonize with each other easily. Effort is required. And the hurt caused towards each other is the price you pay to settle the negative karma created between you and them.

Negative karma is carry forwarded for many births. Karma is like a bank account of actions. You have a credit and a debit account. Whatever good goes to your credit balance and whatever bad you do becomes a debt.

The account is managed throughout your life and also gets carry forwarded to next births (if you believe in reincarnation). Everyone has to pay the debts and earn the reward of their good actions whether they want/like it or not.

The Growth Time of Actions:
The Universal Law of Karma works in a very deep and subtle way. Not every action is rewarded or punished immediately or in the same birth. Action is like a seed; say a mango seed will take around 4-5 years to become a complete mango tree whereas a rose plant will bloom with roses in weeks. Likewise, the consequences of our actions have their own reap period.

Immediate Cause and Effort:
Some of our actions produce effects immediately where we realize this is what caused it.

There is an easy recognition of the result.

Example: You don't study well for a semester exam; you fail and you know it all.

Past Births Karmic Effort:

Other events occur as a result of actions from our previous births which we do not identify. Therefore we become annoyed, blame the person causing trouble, the situations, nature or even God for all our problems.

Our memory of one birth is merged in the soul when we leave the body and move on to another birth but the impressions of our actions' effect do stay in the soul. The soul carry forwards the karmic accounts to the next birth.

How to identify the type of Karma:

Past Karma (both good and bad) is what situations comes towards you. New Karma is what you do with it — your response to it. You can either settle or aggravate it.

Classic example of this: Say someone yells at you for no reason (Past Karma coming back to you). If you respond with patience and stay calm — You settle your old debt of sorrow (from the subdivision debt of anger).

There are different types of sorrow:

- sorrow from negative emotions, e.g., jealousy, anger, fear
- physical pain from bodily disease
- sorrow from mental issues
- sorrow caused from loss
- sorrow from relationships

- sorrow from natural calamities
- sorrow from unavailability of basic needs — food, clothing and shelter
- sorrow due to financial difficulties

All the above types of sorrow fall under various subdivisions of debt. The debt collector is the energy of the Universal Law of Karma who delivers events, situations, problems, natural calamities to collect the various debts from the world's souls in their entire life.

Hmmm... seems like a heavy dose right?

Take a deep breath!

There is always light in the end of life's tunnel — if not in one birth but there is definitely light in the end of all the births. Getting puzzled?

How to remove invisible curtains and become light from the burdens of negative karma?

1. Identify the invisible curtains around you.
2. Accept them.
3. Understand from my heart that it is not the person in front of me causing sorrow; but my own unsettled old debt.
4. Take responsibility of all your past and present actions.
5. Don't react but rather give love, care, tolerance, forgiveness, patience, happiness and peace to the person and situation.
6. Don't prove/fight/blame anyone.
7. Don't become a victim.

8. Increase your credit balance, i.e., positive actions.
9. Embrace the negative matters and transform them with an attitude of happiness that your baggage is reducing; your debts are getting cleared.
10. I am becoming lighter and lighter. My meetings with my debt collectors will reduce, i.e., people giving problems.

All this knowledge is given to bring one into lightness and awareness and not to feel upset about all the negative karma one has made. The truth is each soul in this world has heavy baggage and numerous invisible curtains. You are not alone!

You may not see it explicitly in your life as most of the baggage is subtle and invisible. Only that soul knows it. The Universal Law of Karma is a beautiful law; it keeps the justice in the world in an invisible manner. But to understand the law; patience is essential.

Be aware of it. Embrace it and Do Good!

Note: There is lot of depth in the Law of Karma, this session just covered the basic. If you like to learn more, you can contact our BK Meditation centers. Details are available at the end of the book. Also, it's completely all right if you do not agree with the Karmic Laws, the concept is to be positive and do good.

Om Shanti (I am peace)

How To Handle Anxiety In Family Gathering

Birthday/Wedding parties? Thanksgiving/Christmas Eve/New year Eve? Or even a simple visit of family relatives?
You find Anxiety in the air!
Do you get nervous, worried, tensed and have sleepless nights? Welcome to the Club of Anxiety members!

Women undergo more anxiety when compared to men in terms of family gatherings. What is making me anxious? What is making me worried?
"Fear" Does it ring a bell?

- Fear of people's critics
- Fear of gossip
- Fear of losing my image
- Fear of getting rejected
- Fear of judgement

Drilling down further, the fear of all the above is connected to the deepest fear of losing one's self-dignity and love.

The Scene:
Sometimes you do get uncomfortable to be smiling and be in best behavior continuous for three to four hours. It becomes a stress to put on this act if it is not natural. Everyone in the gathering is trying to show case their good deeds, best

costumes, jewelry, advertising their recent accomplishments, children's activities and much more.

People do this because they want you to create a good image about them in the listener's mind like "I want you to think highly about me." Through the crowd's applause, exclamation, wonder and praise, they feed their ego. They seek pride, fame and honor in disguise. You get anxious when you are unable to do such marketing and advertising of yourself and your family. You are just not comfortable in acting with false masks.

For introverts, it's even more challenging because they are unable to come out from their cocoon or silent nature. Adding to it, some have fear getting rejected by others. Out of immense courage when they do speak out their first word of sharing or a comment, and it is criticized by family members, Boom! They get deeply hurt and go back to their cocoon (quiet mode).

That's why most people dislike family gatherings because they are afraid of being judged by others. Most of them drive back home full of hurt, disturbed and feeling a sense of lack of self-worth proposed and proved by others to you.

Different Modes of Anxiety:
If you are an anxious person, in order to protect your being you either go to attack mode or victim mode in a gathering. Attack mode souls, in order to defend themselves, start playing the game of putting people down, taunting, gossiping so that they don't become a victim.

They do get nervous before the gathering but they make up themselves to avoid being teased or criticized.

Internally they know it's wrong; but they still do it as they feel they have no choice. Such souls do accumulate the karma of causing sorrow.

Victim mode:

They do not want to attack; in other words they do not want to comment, criticize or gossip but just be there, play low. Eventually since they are quiet, they might get attacked and become victims.

Handling Anxiety: Cool Mode

I dress up my soul in cool mode for the party.

Neither be in attack nor victim mode.

Dress Up One:

- I do it by not feeding my self-worth from others.
- I let go of my public image; I let go of what people think about me.
- I remove my expectations of feeling good by praise or fame.
- I create love and respect for myself.
- I become powerful; empowered from within.
- I naturally blend in with everyone. Meeting everyone becomes quite easy and natural as I am coming from a different space now.

Dress Up Two:

- Consider each meeting as a chance for giving and not taking.

- I am not here to take any approval, recognition, love, greetings and honor from any soul in this gathering.
- I am here to give.
- I am hosting or attending this to give something and learn something new.
- Pick up qualities and virtues just like picking up fragrant flowers in a beautiful garden.

Dress Up Three:
- I develop openness and embrace everyone as they are.
- I smile from my heart.
- I talk a few words of sweetness whenever there is side track of gossip or negative comments.
- I display a gentle gesture of silence and tactfully change the topic or guide my group into different conversation without being abrupt. I should not do it from the place of hurt or dislike because people might catch that feeling and counter attack.

Preparation before the Gathering:
- Prepare your mind before every event.
- Hold on to your inner power.

I visualize all the people I am going to meet and the place I am attending or hosting the gathering. I send peace and love to them in advance. I recall their faces and send peace. This mental rehearsal will form a subtle connection between you and them and harmonize your real interaction.

Because you have prepared the soil(mind), when you are in person with them, the planting of your good thoughts or words will yield a positive fruit (result). I do make an extra effort with whom I have the most challenge.

All fear dissolves with positive mental workouts.

Reflection:
1. Have you experienced anxiety in your family gathering? Write two examples.
2. Apply the 3 dress-up solutions to a past or present anxious situation. Check how much were you able to do it and whether the percentage of anxiety reduces.

Om Shanti (I am peace)

Parents and Teenagers - Parents Page

Some parents question,
Why is not my son/daughter listening to me?
Why are they avoiding me?
Why don't they come to me and spend some time?
Why don't they share what is happening in their lives?
I want them to be safe; be on time to the house, but they don't understand.

Some of the issues which parents usually face with teenagers are,

*   Laziness and carelessness. Some teenagers don't realize the seriousness and are playful. They do not have value for the time, money and the effort parents make on them.

*   Having no goal in life

*   Bad company.

*   Lack of responsibility and respect towards parents.

Parents learn more about themselves when they bring up a child. It is a lifelong relationship to be cared for. In this session we will discuss some solutions parents can practice in their relationship with sons and daughters.

Appreciation and Encouragement:
Example: Once a father asked his son to paint the fence. When the boy finished it, the father went to look at the fence along with his son. He observed there were two spots that were not painted properly. Being disappointed, he immediately pointed those spots to his son and asked his son

to repaint it and left with an upset face. Later that evening, the son went up to his father sitting in the couch and said: "Dad, I painted the fence. But why weren't you able to see the rest of the fence that was painted well?" Whenever you ask your children to do something, develop the habit of acknowledging, appreciating and encouraging them.

Our eyes immediately go to the mistakes they have made rather than looking at their good work.

We should be happy at least my son/daughter moved the trash outside even though he/she placed it in the wrong place. Of course we have to correct, educate them and point out their mistakes but before that, we have to appreciate the task they have done correctly and then with love and pure wishes, we can suggest the corrections.

Suggestions are better than instructions and orders. Alter your tone of ordering to suggestion and request. Sometimes parents feel that their kids have to obey them forever. But obeying should come from the place of love and understanding. If your children are obeying to you by force, then today they might obey because they are dependent on you, but later in their lives, they may not respect you.

It doesn't mean that we allow them to commit mistakes, be lazy, careless and get spoiled. No, we establish a relationship of understanding, friendliness, love, respect and discipline. It has to be built over years.

Discipline is taught by a mixture or balance of love and firmness/strictness.

Example: We can teach good manners through explaining to them with love and patience. Explanation is necessary for everything you ask them to do because they want a logical answer. The younger generation is more intellectual henceforth they cannot blindly follow the orders. Providing explanations will help them to follow you.

But if they still don't do it, you can use a timeout/grounding/ cutting their allowance which will enable them to understand the consequences of bad manners. But never use force because they will rebel and throw tantrums.

Trust and Freedom:
We need to trust our children. Most parents at one point have fear and doubt their teenage boys and girls. We need to develop a sense of respect and trust towards our children as they grow up.

They are also young beings living in this world of stress growing towards their maturity and interpreting the world to their best ability. Teenagers experience a phase from their childhood to maturity both physically and mentally. So we need to treat them as equals, not like kids.

The more you listen and trust them, the more they will be open with you. You need to understand that your son/ daughter also knows what is right and wrong, thinking and planning about his/her life.

We have to step back and provide the freedom and space. Suggest and let it go. Give them their space and a sense of freedom to do what they like (within limits). Do not micromanage. When you are a portrait of your guidance, they will automatically come to you for support and guidance. When they do come to you, be a friend and talk to them, do not use authoritative mode or "I said so" tone.

We need to understand that, "I am not the controller of my son/daughter's life, they have their own script to play and I am there to support them if they need me".

Friendly Relationship:
Your quality of relationship with your children is vital as they become teenagers. As parents, we need to change our angle and view, to see them as mature men or women rather than seeing them as kids. We no longer need to run behind them for every little thing or do things for them (spoiling them with too much love and care). The training period is when they are kids. Real parenting is to train them to be independent by the time they become teenagers.

We need to change our behavior and be more friendly:
- Showing interest in their friends and contacts.
- Encouraging their goals and dreams.
- Suggesting and discussing rather than commanding.
- Sharing some matters of work and family so that they feel they are treated as adults.

- Getting their ideas, opinions and involving them in your family decisions. When they feel they are given importance, they will take up responsibility.

A friendly relationship is also necessary for parents in order to understand the peer pressure from other children at school in the level of culture, environment, friends, contacts, money, material things, gadgets and appearance. The kids don't open up to their parents easily because they are afraid of their reaction. A friendly relationship will help a lot in this aspect.

Be an Example:
In this technological world, children no longer look up to their parents for knowledge. They have access to the entire knowledge of the world through the Internet. Children nowadays are intellect based. They have daily examples of sharp, smart, successful intellectual people in front of them but what they lack is an example of love, courage, perseverance and positivity.

Therefore children will look up to parents and respect them only when they become an example of positive virtues and powers. When you are always calm in every situation, your son or daughter will learn from you automatically. They will listen to you when you guide them not to fight or argue because they would see you as an embodiment of calmness.

If you only say and not do, they will ignore you.
Become an understanding parent who gently guides their children to the right path by being an example.

Reflection:

1. Write five specialties and three weaknesses of your children.
2. Write three action points to develop a friendly relationship with your teenager.
3. With an honest heart, write how much you do what you teach to your teens?

Om Shanti (I am peace)

Parents and Teenagers - Teenagers Page

It is said that you cannot choose your parent or child but they are given to you as a gift. It is essential to learn to appreciate the gift and preserve it.

Teenagers:

- Why are my parents always behind me?
- Why they are always telling me what to do? Why do they try to control me?
- Why can't they let me do what I want? Give me some freedom.
- Why do they lecture me?
- They never appreciate/thank me!
- Why do they keep ignoring my opinions/ideas/suggestions, e.g., putting me down?
- I know what I am doing...I am a grown up!

The first and foremost relationship you get in your life is with your parent. You can never forget your childhood. It stays with you till the end of your life. Believe it or not, everyone under goes a bitter phase in their childhood in one way or another. It is not visible yet each of us know the truth inside.

Being a teenager or young adult, it is normal to have the above feelings. On one hand, it is the reality that I am undergoing the stress of being controlled but on the other hand, I can allow myself to learn, become mature and handle the situation.

Rather than feeling being victimized, I can take charge of my feelings and I can change the world around me through my perception.

Understanding My Parents:
Whenever they do anything to me, I need to understand where my parents are coming from. Why they are behind me?
The simple answer is "Love" and "Fear." My parents love me and they want the best for me and the best of me. They are afraid or worried about me, my future and my behavior.

When I understand their intention, it is easy for me to deal with them. The feeling of "running away from the house as soon as possible", "avoiding parents' lecture, phone calls and texts" will not appear. Being a teenager, it might be difficult to handle 24 hour vigilance from parents, but I can always change the vigilance if I don't play games with them and let them know "I am safe."

Another hitch in letting them know my plans is their advice and control regulations on me regarding late nights, parties, field trips and so on. Thereby I am forced to tell lies and create stories to do what I want. I have no other option. They are not going to understand my spirit to enjoy, my friends, my joy and happiness.

Yes, absolutely right but I can avoid this falsehood if I work on my relationship with my parents. First of all, Am I ready to do this? Irrespective of how my parents are, I can make this work according to me.

Again all my effort and success depends on,

- Past and current quality of my relationship with my parents.
- Family environment.
- The personality of my parents.
- Me.

Though it is a mutual effort, I know a very basic rule of life is that I may not be able to change the people and environment around me but definitely I rule my own life and I can change me.

So coming back to falsehood, I can always negotiate with my parents. One tip is parents would definitely allow you to pursue your joys and choices when you take responsibility at the house. When you help them with the household chores, naturally any parent will be happy to listen to you and give your freedom. But I need to do it sincerely and not for the sake of bargaining my freedom with them.

Developing Respect for Elders and Parents:
This might seem traditional in this modern age but respect in terms of knowing and listening to each other.
My parents advise me because,

- They want me to be happy.
- They do not want me to repeat the mistakes they have done.
- They are experienced which means that since they have seen the world 20 or 30 years before me, I need to give some value for that experience.

What can I do?

- I need not obey but at-least listen what they are saying.
- I need not heed their words but give a genuine regard to their word.
- I need not agree but just accept.
- I need not argue but discuss my views when they are in good mood.

When I reject someone immediately, they get hurt. They will be unable to see my logic and intention as my rejection and anger is clouding their intellect. So, let me sit and convey my feelings in a calm and polite manner. If I get angry, let me resolve my anger personally and then go and speak with them.

I can create a harmonious relationship with my parents. Once I win their hearts, all my reasonable requests will be approved.

- Let me value my beautiful parents
- Let me learn from them.
- Let me appreciate all they have done for me since I was born.
- Let me love and respect their care and attention on me.
- I accept them along with their flaws after all they are also human beings trying to do their best.

Om Shanti (I am peace)

How Women Give Difficulty To Other Women

There are great and beautiful relationships between women like mother-daughter, sister-sister, and friend-friend. Similarly there are some relationships between women where they give a hard time to each other like colleague-colleague, mother in law and daughter in law, sister in law and daughter in law.

Today we are going to focus on such relationships and how to handle difficult women. Let's list some of the difficulties women face with other women,

- being rude with each other
- not providing opportunities (at workplace)
- comparison, criticism and complaining about other woman's good work/talents
- revenge, grudge includes the planning and execution of it
- gossip and a lot of gossip
- judgment stares — basically the way they look at you
- making the other woman feel low as if she means nothing

A woman gives a hard time to another woman due to various reasons. Some of them are listed here,

Jealousy:
When a woman finds another woman as her competitor or opponent, she kind of starts an emotional war with her.

When she finds that the other is:

- more beautiful (externally) than she
- more talented than she
- more loved by everyone than she
- more successful than she
- Luckier than she

Why is she jealous of her?
Because she is afraid that the other woman can:

- Replace her.
- Take away her popularity, name and fame.
- Cause people to ignore her and go to this other woman at house/work — Fear of getting rejected or ignored.
- To show and feel that she is important and no one can be as important as her.

Example: An Indian mother in law feels insecure when a new daughter in law comes in. When she sees the daughter in law is smart and gets everyone's love and attention from the members of the home, she feels being left out and she makes her stand in the family to control the daughter in law.

She can be attached to her image of being loved or regarded. She is not willing to share that love or respect with the other woman even though she knows that the other woman deserves it.

It is just her inability to accept and share; she becomes a rebel and works against the other woman at family/work. The beautiful relationships between women are the ones with those who come to rescue the woman facing difficulty with other women by supporting and encouraging her.

Example: Only the mother/sister/friend supports, understands and guides her daughter in her relationship with the mother in law.

Only a woman friend helps another woman who is having a hard time with her woman boss. The reason is women understand the psychology of women better than men.

Fear of Losing her Image/Position/Value and Insecurity: When a woman employee is promoted or even appreciated for her work at workplace, she attracts three types of reaction:

- Those who are her friends feel happy for her.
- Those who don't like her that much feel alarmed by this act of praise and start giving her a hard time(includes gossip, envy and little negative acts of damaging that appreciation)
- Egoistic Men.

When a woman cannot express her feelings directly, she gossips. She unburdens her heavy heart in this process and most women love this process. As women tend to work with their feelings more than men, they easily take things personally. Instead of feeling happy for her colleague, she might compare herself and feel jealous.

It's her fear and insecurity that drives her to be mean. Women also tend to create groups and isolate other women who don't get along with them. This especially happens at schools. The girls who are sidelined develop a low self-esteem as they feel a whole gang is against them.

Projection:
Say a woman had to handle a mean lady boss in her early work years. Eventually when she becomes the boss, she may project that meanness and frustration towards her woman subordinates. Not all women do that but some do.

Whenever we face hardships; being bossed around, bullied, exploited, treated meanly and rude by others, disrespected in our lives, we all have two choices:
- I can make a determined decision that I will never give such hardship to anyone!
- Subconsciously or consciously – I can download the same hardship to another victim.

Women tend to do this projection without realizing that they are trapping themselves in the karma of suffering.

Discontentment and Doubt:
You can never ever make a woman content because no matter how much you do, she will always find something missing/faulty/better.
Example: You do great work at your work and everyone appreciates it except this woman colleague as she finds one or another fault with it.
Example: You clean the house so well yet your mother in law feels you can still keep your spices organized better in the kitchen.
Women also have the habit of doubting and do not develop trust easily. The habit of doubting in a way to be cautious and

to protect oneself but at the same time to be always doubtful doesn't provide happiness.

Women cannot always make up their minds due to the habit of doubt. You know how the shopping episode runs!

How to handle a hard-time-giving woman at work?
- Keep up your self-esteem. Meditate daily.
- You cannot change anyone but you can alter your attitude, thoughts and feelings.
- Be strong and believe in yourself.
- Whatever they say is only their opinion so do not give value to it.
- You keep doing your work; truth and honesty always pays back.
- Do not hate them or consider them as your enemies but develop mercy and good wishes for them.
- They are giving you a hard time due to their own inner weakness or even projecting their hurt to you. So do not take it personally.
- At such times, be in your own world. Do not pay attention to the negative environment.
- Wear a genuine smile. Do not give a stern face or a long face. This might trigger them to trouble you more.
- Make friends with them if possible. If not, stay strong and powerful that your powerful thoughts keep you protected.
- Do not perceive her as an enemy or hold any grudge as this only poisons your heart and if you do, you will become a difficult woman yourself.

- Have empathy for those women. Probably they are simply projecting their weaknesses towards you.

- Be kind and respectful to them as you can be an example of a strong positive woman.
- Lend them a helping hand whenever possible at work especially around men. This might help the woman to see how you are on her side.
- Appreciate her good work with a sincere heart.

How to treat other women with love and respect?
Women are in the same boat at most places. Therefore it's necessary to protect each other from polluting environment. When women stay united and respectful to each other, a lot of unsaid troubles can be avoided. No one can get betrayed and walked upon when women stand up for each other.

Each woman is a source of power and unique in her own beautiful way. Each woman is as beautiful as the other both within and outside.

- Let women love and care for every woman in her family, school, work and society.

- Let each woman raise her voice for other woman whenever help is needed.

- Let a woman not show her anger, frustration and fear towards another woman as she is already facing the same from some other end.

- Let a woman not consider another woman as an opponent but an ally.

- Let women strengthen the bond of womanhood and have each other's back.

- Let women built trust, harmony and friendship with each other.

Reflection:
1. Do you give difficulty to any woman in your life? If so, can you transform your attitude?
2. Appreciate every woman you live/work with. Share her positivity with others in your circle today.

Om shanti(I am peace)

Fear at Workplace

At work, sometimes you sense your role has become mellow or ordinary in your perception and others' role comes in lime light. Everyone is praising and speaking about them. The feel you get is like the nonstop talk about the latest movie in the radio. And when you see that sudden glow for the people around you, do you feel comfortable?

Colleagues and peers are getting more attention than you because of an accomplishment such as an excellent marketing ad or a great project proposal. Here you are, sitting in the same chair; doing the same work (you do quality work); but no one notices and on top of it seeing the pomp; you feel insecure, unworthy and irritated.

The truth is all the pomp and show lasts only for a specific time slot; once other new things come, new or other employees receive the attention. People who come in the limelight are constantly changing.

If you observe, you will find a cycle of change. Of course there are some people who are always popular because of their sweet friendly nature. Ignoring this secret of cycle, we tend to prove or try constantly to keep up our name/fame and destroy our health, family time and peace of mind in the process. We tend to fight to gain a place, to be praised by everyone, to be the talk of the town and how everyone should think that I am great.

All this will happen but the question is "Is it worth it?" "Does it truly give you happiness?" Because people will praise you today and tomorrow insult you too. Are you ready to take both? So it is better to keep focus and be content with our own being and carry on. You do your duty and let go of the result. It will come back to you in a graceful manner.

Inner Fear can be removed when,
1.   I understand each one of us will come in the lime light one day.

So when my colleagues or friends come in lime light, I am happy for them. No one has come to take anything from me. Even if they want to, according to Karmic Law, they cannot take. It might seem like taking but realistically it's not. It is just my fear blaming the other person taking away my peace of mind.

Example: You may think that someone is a threat to your job position. But the truth is it is not possible until you allow it even though they want to grab it from you.

If you lose hope and constantly feel the threat and create thoughts that so and so is going to take your position, eventually it will happen because your thoughts invited and created the situation.

Always remember positive feelings are more powerful than mental and intellectual energy.

But if you are clear and confident about your creativity, talent, skill set and experience, nothing can beat you!

The Golden Law: Everything Comes and Goes!

Praise, Name, Fame, Money, and Position comes and goes. It moves from one hand to another hand. There is nothing to lose in this world because nothing belongs to you eternally anyway. You are worthy of respect always. Nothing can add or reduce your value.

People and Materials come to you for a purpose and when it is fulfilled they leave you naturally.

This may sound difficult to practice, but at least if I could feed these thoughts to my mind, it might reduce my suffering momentarily. Raja Yoga helps us to practice this golden law. Gradually and eventually one can lead a worry free life.

2. At times, life will bring the strengths in me and at times my weaknesses; so I cannot judge myself or others based on my response to the situation. I keep myself still and see the situation come and go passing by me.

Example: Say a certain situation brings up your feeling of insecurity buried inside you, it appears in the screen of your mind repetitively and you will be wondering what is happening with you, why do you feel insecure all of a sudden?

- Don't panic or get worried.
- Take it easy.
- Detach and observe the environment and yourself.

You could notice a person/an incident/an old friend/discussion of last night party/movie/even a memory of something triggered your emotion of insecurity or that fear.

Once you realize that fear is a temporary trigger, you can easily get rid of it. Fear can be replaced by clarity, self-confidence, courage, hope and easiness.

Reflection:
1. Am I attached to my image, name and position at work?
2. Can I be happy and appreciative to my colleagues whenever they receive something I don't receive?
3. If not, uncover the reasons and why not resolve them.

Om shanti(I am peace)

Healing in Relationships

Healing is like a medicine for the soul. We all have lots of wounds and scars in our souls like bad memories, guilty feeling of our own bad actions, unforgivable actions of others, huge damage or loss, unrecoverable health or accidents, betrayal, cruel and brutal behavior, abuse, merciless attitude of others, worse childhood memories and much more. They continuously haunt us and suck our spiritual power out.

The occurrences of the above events cannot be stopped or controlled by anyone but healing is completely in our hands. There are various ways of healing:
- Healing through your inner beauty
- Healing through time
- Healing through the Divine/God
- Healing through understanding
- Healing through faith
- Healing through forgiveness, mercy and compassion

In this session, we will see how healing in relationships happens by using a quick recovery time of our emotions and actions.

Recovery Time or Rollback power:
Recovery time is the time to recover our self to the normal state of peace, love and happiness from a disturbance. Problems come but how long is our recovery time?

All of us make mistakes. They cannot be stopped. No matter how much you yell, explain or have close supervision, mistakes happen. People repeat mistakes again and again and you go again and again shouting, yelling, complaining, and frustrated...Wait a minute. This cycle is endless. The only way to stop this cycle is to accept that things happen. It's okay. Can I recover myself immediately?

Example: forgetting the car key

Reaction 1: Your sister forgot to get the car key before locking the house, it's okay, not a big deal, extra few minutes delay, it is fine, and acceptance of the scene that drama is revealing to you. Smile and let your sister get the key. Forget it, take it easy, let it go and enjoy the pleasant drive. Acceptance and accommodating one another will help me to not make mistakes a big deal.

Reaction 2: You frown, complain or get mad at your sister for putting both of you in a bad mood and there goes your drive with dead silence in the car. The vibes of the car are full of the emotions like dislike, discontentment that messes up the whole day. You don't stop there, you start recalling all the mistakes that your sister has made so far and you burden your heart further.

Example: "You always forget....You are always clumsy..."

Healing never happens this way, only scars are created. The old scars are pricked further, leading to suffering and taking us into an unforgivable mode. We enter this mode because we have the habit of connecting one mistake with past mistakes, which makes our suffering so huge that we are unable to forgive it. We also feel it's too much to tolerate and that they deserve this treatment.

But who made a small mistake larger?

It's me! I can make a poppy seed into a mountain or a mountain into a cotton wool. I have that power. Let me use the same power to make bigger things smaller.

Recovery Time Process:

Something happens, you react — you yell/become upset/ depressed/mood-off/tensed and quarrel or whatever it's okay... but after that part of you finishes, you are becoming normal again in few minutes/hours/days. This is called recovery time. This time varies for each individual.

Some people do the above reactions but the miserable part is, they get stuck there for hours/days/months and even years. A difference of opinion or misunderstanding happens between two people, one gets angry and the other gets angry, quarreling for 5-10 minutes, okay no problem, but after 15 minutes or even hours, be back to normal — smile, talk again and be as if nothing happened.

It is part of life and the flow of relationships to allow hiccups but to take it light and easy. No matter what happens, there should not be any,

- break-up
- distance
- cold war
- silent treatment

You may fight 1000 times a day, doesn't matter, at the end of the day the relationship stays intact, i.e., love, sweetness, smiles, sharing, eating food together, doing things for each other.... Because relationships are created based on a special understanding between two souls and it has been built on love, forgiveness, good memories, sharing, time spend together, things enjoyed together...and they will never go away, no matter what happens. A mother will always remain a mother to her child, nothing can change it.

Similarly a spouse is always a spouse or any relationship; a bond of understanding is established... Nowadays if anything happens say a small fight, we tend to go to extreme like "I will not talk to you forever," "Let's break up," "I hate you; don't see me anymore."

We just cut the relationship without even communicating directly by making false excuses.

It does not mean that you should suffer always and not end any relationship. It depends on you, your tolerance level, how much you value a relationship. But the above aspects are just an angle of looking at relationship conflicts.

Healing takes place through this speedy recovery time. When I smile again or talk again to the person I had the problem with, there is a higher chance for him/her to be normal again. If you observe children, they have beautiful recovery time, they never take anything seriously among their friends group, if one comes back and says sorry or just talk again, they quickly accept, embrace him and continue having fun.

They do not fight like adults in terms of ego. As the clock is ticking, let's heal our relationships through understanding, loving, respecting each other and giving support to our loved ones when they need us and not to leave them alone at their time of need. This is why we are given family and friends!

Reflection:
1. Does your heart carry open wounds? List three wounds that needs to be healed to create a peaceful and loving heart.
2. Apply forgiveness and try to take responsibility to heal those wounds. Explore the details.
3. Write your recovery time, i.e., how much time does it take for you to become peaceful after a conflict?

Om Shanti (I am peace)

Coping with Sadness - Life After Losing One's Spouse

When life hits us with sudden tragic incidents like losing one's spouse, life turns out to be hard on us. Suddenly you become alone. The house becomes empty and whatever was handled together or by your spouse has to be handled by only you now.

On top of it, you have to handle all the memories that hit you time to time. The things in the house that remind you constantly of the person you lived with. You feel sorry for yourself and why you have been rendered upon with such misery. You start to compare your life with that of others and feel unfortunate.

Life turns out to be cruel and lonely especially when you are in the age group where your kids are grown up and away from you. You are in your later part of your life without your life partner and you feel that you are just passing life. Another concern is also on health. To handle your health issues on your own and to keep up the courage to execute all the practical routine of life.

Example: Your spouse used to always accompany you to your doctor appointments and now you have to undertake that journey on your own.

Having described the situation above, there are few things which can be done to live life without sadness.

Accepting the Situation:

Things could have happened suddenly like losing your spouse in an accident or a gradual loss through disease. In the latter case, your mind gets kind of prepared but in the former case, the mind is in shock of the sudden loss of the person who was your support and companion. In either case, acceptance of the loss helps.

How to Accept?

- I am grateful to have known this special person(your spouse) in my life and spent precious years with him/her.
- My marriage was a journey and it was time for my partner to move on with his stop. I have learned many things from my partner to continue my journey further.
- The soul is eternal and imperishable. Only the body dies, soul is immortal. My spouse is always with me in spirit.
- I am grateful for all the lovely memories with my spouse that I can always cherish. I recollect those memories with gratitude and happiness not with regret and sadness.
- Everyone has to leave their bodies one day including myself. So I respect the law of nature and call upon my courage to accept this nature.
- I still have to continue to play my role in this life. I have the capacity to run my life as a powerful individual using my life to its better purpose.

Embrace Life:
There are some situations where you are not healthy and dependent upon others. This could be depressing and make you miss your spouse even more.

When you are dependent on your friends /relatives/nurses for your daily needs, the heart does becomes heavy and make you feel purposeless. There is a kind of disinterest that creeps in, making your life tasteless and feel miserable questioning even your very existence.

Here is where one has to use one's courage and hope in life.
- I am alive to fulfill my purpose whatever that might be.
- The universe has kept me alive for a good cause in spite of health issues.
- I have been given the power to handle them too.
- I need to allow my power to emerge as I move on.
- I can be a good source of guidance and wisdom to my children, grandchildren and friends.
- I could do things which I couldn't do earlier due to my family commitment.
- Life has given me a new chance to live and the freedom to explore options.
- Let me embrace it with hope rather than getting stuck in the past.

Do Good Karma, Pursue Pending Projects and Dreams:
I can use it as an opportunity to be good with others who help me with my needs. I can also resume my paused projects and dreams. I can develop a new hobby or a project to give

direction to my mind. I use my time to benefit others and serve the community. I can get connected with support groups who empower and do things together with them.

Company of God:
I can also use the company of God to ease me with my pain and suffering. No one is alone in the company of God. God is always with us.

We just forget it and go far away seeking human being's company. God is beyond time and space therefore He can give me 24 hours company and be available for me at any place. I need not feel alone rather I can call upon God's company in a relationship say friend/mother/spouse.
I can share everything with God and He will listen to me.
You will also receive responses and you will be amazed with that. God always hears the whispers made to Him with a true heart.

Hatha Yoga and Meditation:
Another good way to get rid of your lonely feelings and build self-confidence and interest in life is to get involved in Hatha Yoga and Meditation. You can try some stretching, breathing and postures based on your health which will give comfort and healing energy to your body. Meditation helps your mind to relax, stay peaceful and focused. Raja Yoga meditation helps you to master your mind and create a positive relationship with yourself, others and life.

How to cope up and find purpose in life after loss?
By taking it as a learning process to live life on my own. I am learning and it is a sort of adventure to come out of my comfort zone and face the world.
Example: I learn how to pay my bills. I figure out things with the help of my friends and the Internet. Rather than feeling left out, I seek out and drive the energy towards learning and new experience.

To call upon my inner strength and courage to go and do the chores.
Example: You would have been a housewife and did not have any experience of the outside world earlier. But now the challenge is to come out of the shell and take care of both in-house and out-door activities.

Buying grocery, plumbing (In some cultures, men do all the outside work including grocery shopping and women take care of the house only). So it becomes a challenge for such women to step out of the house and handle those activities after losing their partners. Rather than becoming dependent and feeling self-pity, I become independent and use my then received freedom in empowering my life and that of others. You get plenty of time for yourself.

Ask yourself what are some of the desires/passions which you couldn't fulfill since you started your family life.
Example: Learning a music instrument, writing a book, teaching at kindergarten, singing, joining a gym, exercise, travel and community projects.

If you are a working person, you could involve yourself more at work for a certain period until your mind recovers. If you are interested, you can invest time in spirituality and devotion. Do something on a regular basis like yoga, meditation, visiting temples/churches/mosques/meditation centers regularly. Join a social club like a women's club or any other social organization for community service. The idea is to divert the mind that is caught up in the past and give life a new purpose.

When I get involved in the above activities, I can find new meaning to life. After all, life is not only to create and sustain a family life, it is much more than that. I can also consider this single life as an opportunity to explore life in a bigger perspective like investing my time and energy in benefiting others.

I need to broaden my mind from a small family cluster thinking to a global thinking. Our lives are valuable and I am a valuable person in this world. I can bring transformation and be an example to inspire others even in a small way.
I can be a symbol of courage to someone. I can be a good guide/educator to someone. I can use my skills and talents and benefit others. This life is a great way to express your inner being to its fullest potential.

So Get Up and Live Your Life!

Om shanti (I am peace)

About the Author

Padmapriya Mahendarkar Alias Sister Priya is the Meditation Center Coordinator of the Brahma Kumaris, St. Louis branch and a Raja Yoga meditation practitioner since 2002.

She has Bachelors in Information Science and Masters of Business Administration and has worked in the Telecom industry at India for eight years. At 2009, she dedicated her life with the Brahma Kumaris and became a full fledged Raja Yoga teacher in USA.

Since then she has been facilitating self development classes and workshops for people from all walks of life. Her classes are simple, engaging and motivational. Her guided meditation commentaries are soothing and provides deep experiences to the listener.

Sister Priya is the author of "100 Inspirational Thoughts Part 1" and "The Incredible Power Within" books. For any questions on the book, feel free to email at bksisterpriya@gmail.com

About the Brahma Kumaris

The Brahma Kumaris World Spiritual Organization acknowledges the intrinsic goodness of all people. They teach a practical method of meditation that helps individuals understand their inner strengths and values.

A worldwide family of individuals from all walks of life, they are committed to spiritual growth and personal transformation, believing it to be essential in creating a peaceful and just world.

The Brahma Kumaris World Spiritual University in Mt. Abu, India, is an international non–governmental organization (NGO) in general consultative status with the Economic and Social Council of the United Nations and in consultative status with UNICEF. It is also affiliated to the UN Department of Public Information.

Through its international network of centers, the BK's organize special activities, seminars, workshops, dialogues, conferences, and exhibitions to provide people with spaces to voice their opinions on critical matters that impact their daily lives.

Raja Yoga Meditation

The Raja Yoga Meditation taught by the Brahma Kumaris comprises the three following segments;

Relationship with the Self:
This session provides the BK Teachings on knowing the self, understanding and embracing the strengths and weaknesses of the self. To discover the inner beauty and experience the original virtues of the self. Once the self is understood it paves the way to easy transformation of negative into positive. This session also helps one to understand one's thought patterns, habits and nature.

Relationship with the Source:
This session provides the BK teachings on One Source, the ability and process to tap into the Universal Source of powers. To connect with God without religion but with a direct loving relationship. To experience the spiritual connection between the self and God and recharge the inner self.

Relationship with Karma:
This session provides the BK Teachings on the importance of time and actions. To understand the effect of every action in this world and how to align our thoughts, words and actions. To learn the deep philosophy of Karma and cultivate a natural way of giving happiness and taking happiness in our relationships.

To learn meditation:

To find your local BK center, go to www.us.brahmakumaris.org and look under "Locations."

www.ingramcontent.com/pod-product-compliance
Lightning Source LLC
Chambersburg PA
CBHW060303050426
42448CB00009B/1738